LET WO[MEN] BE WO[MEN]:
EQUALITY, MINISTRY &
ORDINATION

Peter Toon
(M.A., M.Th., D.Phil.)

Gracewing.

Fowler Wright Books
Leominster

Let Women be Women

for
Stratford and Leonie
with thanks
and
in appreciation

CONTENTS

Preface   7

1. Ordain women now!   11

2. The full programme   24

3. An inescapable question   40

4. Ministry and Priesthood   53

5. By whose authority?   66

6. Affirming the masculine   82

7. Celebrating the feminine   97

8. Conclusion   111

Appendix: The proposed legislation for the C. of E.   119

Gracewing.

Fowler Wright Books
2 Southern Avenue
Leominster HR6 0QF

Gracewing Books are distributed

In Canada by
Novalis
PO Box 990
Outremont H2V 457
Canada

In Australia by
Charles Paine Pty
8 Ferris Street
North Parramatta
NSW 2151 Australia

First Published by Fowler Wright Books 1990

All rights reserved. No part of this publication may be reproduced, stored in a retrieval system, or transmitted in any form, or by any means, electronic, mechanical, photocopying, recording or otherwise, without the written permission of the publisher.

© Text Peter Toon 1990
© Excerpts from Man, Woman & Priesthood cited authors
© Cover illustration by Angela Turnbull

ISBN 0 85244 191 6

Typesetting by Print Origination (NW) Ltd, Formby Liverpool L37 8EG
Printed and bound by Billings & Sons Worcester

PREFACE

This is a book which I felt I ought to write but which I did not want to write, because it means I am involved in a controversy about the rights of women and run the risk of being misunderstood and called a male chauvinist! My purpose in writing may be expressed quite simply. It is to invite my reader to consider that the subject of the ordination of women to the presbyterate (= priesthood) cannot stand alone as an isolated topic. We may wish that it could be looked at by itself alone as a subject in its own right but this is not possible. In fact my purpose in writing the book was to reflect theologically on the relationship (established by God in his self-revelation to us) between, on the one hand, the presbyter (= priest) or bishop, and, on the other, three themes – the male identity of our Lord Jesus Christ, the names (e.g. "Father") by which we address the Godhead in our worship, and the equality, dignity and vocation of male and female as creatures made in God's image.

I have tried to produce a non-technical book on a subject keenly debated not only in the Church of England (and Anglicanism generally) but also in the Roman Catholic Church. I have written not for theologians but for those who are discussing this matter at the various levels of decision-making in the Anglican Communion (the local parish and the diocesan and national synods). However, it is my sincere hope that Roman Catholics will also find what I say useful and helpful, for as far as I can judge from my reading of their magazines and newspapers, virtually all I have to say applies very much to their own situation too.

My method is simple. First, I set out as fairly as possible the case for ordaining women as priests/bishops. Secondly, I seek to show the real aims of some of those who are pressing for the ordination of women; and I indicate that their total agenda follows from their arguments for the ordaining of women as priests (not deacons). Thirdly, I reflect on the meaning given to ministry and priesthood in the New Testament. I do this in order to set the topic of ordained ministry in its rich biblical context. Fourthly, I present the case for restricting the orders of priest and bishop to men who are called thereunto by Christ; and I set this case in its own agenda with reflections on patriarchy, the maleness of Jesus, the language we use to address God in worship, and the dignity and ministry of women.

For those who wish to go deeper into the case I have presented I commend *Man, Woman & Priesthood* (ed. James Tolhurst, 1990) which is from the same British publisher as this book. I refer to it several times as *M.W.P.* An even more substantial book worthy of careful study is Manfred Hauke, *Women in the Priesthood?* (Ignatius Press, San Francisco, 1988).

I would also commend *Man and Woman in Christian Perspective* by Werner Neuer (Hodder & Stoughton, 1990).

The title of this book relates it to another book of which I am a co- author: it is *Let God be God* (Darton, Longman & Todd in the UK and Morehouse Publications in the U.S.A., 1989) and it invites readers to let God provide for us the names we use to address him in worship.

I have used the new Revised English Bible in the text. My reason for this is that I believe it represents a sensible attempt to use inclusive language for humanity.

Finally I wish to thank Sheridan Swinson, my editor, for entrusting me with this assignment as well as John Saward, Fred Cape and Vita, my wife, for their help in clarifying my ideas.

Feast of St Peter, Apostle: Peter Toon,
29 June 1990.   Staindrop Vicarage.

CHAPTER 1

Ordain women now!

Let me begin by being open and honest. Often I feel and think that the arguments in favour of ordaining women are persuasive. They are particularly so when presented by an intelligent woman, who is not obviously seeking to make any feminist point and who does not make it her duty to criticise men! I have heard seemingly compelling reasons from both an "ordinationist nun" (a phrase now used by nuns) and a conservative, evangelical female deacon. In such circumstances the doubter can so easily be led to confess: "Yes, I agree; of course women ought to be ordained."

In fact to many people today the question "Should a woman be ordained?" is a non-question for they have answered in the affirmative a long time ago. So they become impatient with those who hesitate or oppose. They believe that unless you are an old-fashioned traditionalist, who wants to preserve things as they are, or a woman-hater, who is against women on principle, then you cannot have any acceptable reason for not wanting to see women ordained.

Setting the scene

Before going any further perhaps we need to be clear what we mean by the "ordination" of women. In the Anglican Church (as also in the Roman and Orthodox Churches) there is a threefold ordained ministry of deacon, presbyter/priest and bishop. Since women are now admitted to the Order of deacons in the Anglican Church, the debate there concerns the other two Orders. Should women be admitted to the Order of priests and to the Order of bishops? Several provinces of the Anglican Communion have already gone ahead, without waiting for the others, and ordained women as both priests and bishops – the American Episcopal Church and the New Zealand Anglican Church are the best known examples.

The Church of England, however, the mother Church of the Communion, is still very much involved in debating the question at all levels, from the parish, through the deanery and diocese to the general synod. Yet due to the generally conservative nature of the Established Church of England only the ordination of women as priests is being considered at this time. If this is eventually accepted in 1992/3 by the General Synod by a two thirds majority and by the British Parliament then perhaps the further question of whether women may also be bishops of the Church and members of the House of Lords will be voted on at the turn of the century. (see the Appendix at the end of this book)

In the Roman Catholic Church there is a vocal, educated minority which is pressing for the ordination of women as deacons and priests. This is often associated with the call for the abolition of the requirement of celibacy for the priesthood. At an official level (within the Vatican and the national hierarchies) there is no interest at all in these proposals however. There the traditional ban on female ordination remains in place. The same is true of the Greek and Russian Orthodox Churches.

The situation within the Church of Scotland (the National Church) and the Free Churches in Britain is somewhat different. They have recently admitted women to the office of pastor and so not a few congregations now have ordained women as their ministers of word and sacrament. Some congregations have a team ministry of a man and his wife, both ordained pastors.

It is now appropriate to ask the question. What reasons do the proponents of female ordination in the Church of England, the Anglican Communion and the Roman Catholic Church give to support their belief that the time has come for making women not only deacons but also presbyters (priests) in God's Church? I have done my very best to hear these and what follows is my summary of the ten I have heard (or read) most frequently. I do not doubt that there are others.

Receiving God's call

First of all there is the argument from religious experience. Not a few mature and intelligent women claim in all sincerity that God has given them an inner call to the ministry of Word and Sacrament. They believe, therefore, that the Church has a duty to test their call (as it does that of men) to preach the Gospel, to preside at the Lord's Table, and to be a pastor of a congregation of Christ's flock. They maintain that if the Church were to test their call by the same criteria used for men at least some of them would go forward to ordination to the priesthood. The fact that they are not allowed even to have their call tested at a selection conference or by the bishop adds to their feeling of being shut out or even oppressed by men in the Church. Further, they feel that men and women who support an all-male priesthood are preventing the work of the Holy Spirit, for it is the Spirit who calls people to sacred office. Further, they do not like to be told that they can be deacons and can find fulfilment in this sacred office. Their call they insist is to the priesthood!

Equal through baptism

In the second place there is that celebrated statement of the apostle Paul. He wrote: "Baptized into union with him, you have all put on Christ like a garment. There is no such thing as Jew and Greek, slave and freeman, male and female; for you are all one person in Christ Jesus" (Gal 3:28). Here, surely, it is emphasised, is a clear declaration of equality in Christ. Through union with Christ, expressed in baptism, the superiority of the Jew and the male is cast aside; in the new covenant God-in-Christ is the Saviour and Lord to Jews and non-Jews, slaves and citizens, and males and females, in exactly the same way. There are no favourites and there is no preference for one or the other. Circumcision in the old covenant was for males only but Christian baptism is for both males and females. If there is such an equality in relationship with God through Christ then, the argument proceeds, there ought to be equality of opportunity of entrance to offices in the Church of God. In short, the presbyterate (priesthood) and episcopate ought to be open to those women who have truly received God's call to be ordained.

Made in God's image

Then, thirdly, there is the great declaration in the first chapter of the book of Genesis. "God created human beings in his own image; in the image of God he created them: male and female he created them."(1:27). There is no sexual discrimination here, for, it is pointed out, we learn that man and woman are made together at the same time by God: they are accorded equal importance; and they are given the double task of bringing children into the world and working together that the world may be a good and fruitful place in which they and their children can live. Working together in partnership both inside and outside of marriage men and women not only discover themselves as human beings but also, even more wonderfully, come to see what it means to be made in God's image. Therefore the argument proceeds, if it is true that God created the human race as male and female in order to reflect his own Being (which according to the doctrine of the Trinity is a trinitarian Being-in- relationship) then this relationship should be reflected in the Church. Thus the priesthood must be open both to male and female for, at the beginning, God "blessed them [MALE and female] and called them man" (Gen 5:2). The conclusion is that a Priesthood without females is impoverished, for it fails to reflect the whole image of God in which humanity is made.

True to the mind of Jesus

In the fourth place, much is made of the example of Jesus himself. In the face of an entrenched discrimination against women, which saw them only as mothers and homemakers without other basic rights, Jesus, it is claimed, took a revolutionary stand. Not only did this teacher from Nazareth show a radically new stance towards women by encouraging them to be his disciples (which a normal Jewish rabbi would never have done), he also confirmed their new position in his teaching. For example Mary, Martha's sister, was commended for not being in the kitchen at the stove, but at the Master's feet like a true disciple (Luke 10:38-42). Further, women were present at the foot of the Cross when Jesus expired and, even more importantly, they were the first witnesses of his resurrection. In fact at the birth of Christianity, on the first Easter Day, it was women who declared to men that Jesus was truly raised from the dead (John 20:1-18; Luke 23:54-24:11)! How strange it is then that women have been forbidden to preach in Christian congregations. Surely if women were the bearers of the Gospel of God concerning Jesus Christ to the apostles, who are the very pillars of the Church, then they should be allowed to preach the Gospel today in the congregation of the faithful! Further, since Jesus left no specific instruction that women could not be his ordained ministers, on what possible grounds, it is asked, can they be debarred from the ordained ministry of the Word and Sacraments?

Truly capable

Fifthly, there is the obvious fact that women have shown that they are capable of all the functions and duties of the ordained ministry. In their recent work as missionaries abroad as well as in parishes, schools, colleges, hospitals and in specialist ministries (e.g. in the inner cities), not to mention work as teachers, lay readers, deaconesses, deacons, administrators, and counsellors, Anglican women (and Catholic women as well) have shown that they can do or in some cases have already done everything that a parish minister is called upon to do. In fact in many cases they have fulfilled these duties with great merit and to the blessing of many people. There is also the experience of women pastors in Protestant denominations who have proved, it is claimed, that women can truly be good ministers of religion. So it is asked with some poignancy. "Is it reasonable to prevent women from being priests when they have shown that they can do well, everything that a priest is called upon to do?"

Genuinely representative

In the sixth place, it is emphasised that the Church ought to learn an important lesson from the world. It is a fact that women are now widely recognised as able to fulfil a representative role in modern nation-states – think of Mrs Indira Gandhi of India, the world's largest democracy, Mrs Golda Meier of Israel with its traditions of male leadership, and Mrs Margaret Thatcher, the "iron-lady" of Great Britain. For the last century or so women have been steadily moving into leadership roles in increasing numbers within western society.

Now to ordain a woman as a presbyter/priest in a situation where a woman is not regarded by the society as being able to fulfil a genuine representative capacity in human society is, it is admitted, to ordain in effect a priestess (with all the overtones of fertility cults and the like). However, to ordain a woman in a society where a woman is seen as being able to be a genuine representative and leader of both men and women is, it is insisted, to ordain a genuine presbyter/priest for God's Church. And since women do now occupy representative positions in society – in government, education, medicine, social services - then there is solid reason why they should occupy them in God's Church, especially when it is borne in mind that male and female are equal in Christ (Gal 3:28). Thus a woman called by God ought to have the opportunity of being a priest, bishop and archbishop, even a pope!

A missionary calling

Seventhly, all admit that there is a massive task facing the Church of God in western society. So much so that the last decade of this century has been named "the Decade of Evangelism" so as to set before the faithful the task of spreading the Gospel within the secularised nations of the West. To take the message of Christ into the world and to embody that message as "lights in the darkness" the Church, it is argued, needs dedicated and representative leaders to guide the whole body of the faithful in its missionary calling and task. However, a leadership in mission which is only male will prove to be a stumbling-block to people in a society which has become accustomed to the equality of men and women in all spheres of life. Thus the point is made that for the sake of the conversion of the world to Christianity, women must be included in the leadership of the mission. In practical terms this means that they must be ordained leaders.

Word and Sacrament belong together

In the eighth place, it is pointed out that in the Eucharist, which is the main service of worship in God's Church, the ministry of the Word and the Sacrament are two parts of one whole. They belong together and must not be prised apart for in and through both, the Holy Spirit makes Christ's presence real to those who attend. Bearing this important truth in mind, the point is made that, at the moment, a woman deacon/deaconess in the Church of England is invited to, and does actually, preach in the Eucharist; but, she is forbidden the privilege of presiding during the ministry of the Sacrament. She can celebrate in the pulpit but not at the Lord's Table! This is, to say the least, an odd state of affairs and can only be put right, it is claimed, by allowing the one who preaches Christ to the flock also to consecrate the divine food of

Christ's body and blood for the same flock. And this requires ordination of the deacon to the priesthood.

Authority to change ordering of ministry

Ninthly, reference is made to the doctrinal confession of the Church of England, the Thirty-Nine Articles. In Article XXXIV it is stated that "Every particular or national Church has authority to ordain, change and abolish ceremonies or rites of the Church ordained only by man's authority, so that all things be done for edifying." From this it is argued that since the ordination of men now is merely "by man's authority" the same "man's authority" can decide to order things differently. In other words a national or particular church can decide to ordain women — as the national churches of Sweden and Norway and Denmark have done. There is no need to wait for the Roman Catholics or for a General Council of the Church to decree the ordination of women.

A development of doctrine

In the tenth place, and finally, it is asserted that God is addressing the Church through the changing culture, and especially the new dignity and freedom which women are experiencing. It is emphasised that this is not the first time that the Church has had to learn an important lesson from events outside itself, rather than from within (listening to God's word). Much is made of the movement to abolish first the slave trade and then slavery itself by the British government in the early nineteenth century. It is claimed that up to that time the Church in general had been content to accept the institution of slavery as part of God's will; the work of William Wilberforce and many others in the political sphere caused the Church to realise that slavery was evil. Thus today few if any Christians would attempt to justify slavery. So, the argument continues, the world is now teaching the Church how to value and use women and in practical terms this means that the Church ought to ordain women as priests immediately. To do such would be a true development of doctrine, bringing into practical reality a seed within the Gospel which has been growing for centuries.

Conclusion

Presented in this simple way there is no doubt, I think, that these ten reasons do as a whole have (at least at first sight and without hearing any arguments against them) a compelling thrust. Anyone whose thinking has been influenced by the general acceptance in western culture of the equal rights of women in education, work, pay and taxation will probably admit that they appear to prove the case for opening immediately all jobs and orders of ministry in the Church to suitably qualified women. But there is more to tell and thus more to reflect upon – see chapter two!

Chapter 2

The full programme

To do justice to many of the women who campaign the hardest for the ordination of women (e.g. the leadership of the Movement for the Ordination of Women), I must now try to explain what I find in their writings and hear in their talks as the context in which their call for women priests and the renewal of the Church is made. They are well educated people whose total agenda is much more than the ordaining of women. They realised some time ago that ordination does not, and cannot, stand alone as a solitary goal. To aim for this goal alone is like aiming for a bull's eye which floats in the air and is not part of the darts' board. Or, to put it another way, they have recognised that achieving only the ordination of women is like buying the engine of a car but not the chassis, the body and the wheels. So they insist with some justification that the ordination of women belongs rightfully and naturally with other developments and changes in the Church if it is to be the means of genuine renewal and advance in God's Church.

What are these developments and changes? First of all, there is the adoption of what is technically called "non-exclusive" and/or "inclusive language" in actual services of worship as well as in all books of liturgies, prayers, and hymnbooks. This development has two aspects: changes in the way we speak of humanity and in how we speak of and address God.

In the second place, there is a new interpretation of the Bible through the acceptance and the use of the doctrine that patriarchy (male domination of women) is evil. Reading the Bible on the assumption that patriarchy is evil can and does lead to radical results, which have immediate reference to traditional Christian doctrine and ethics. In the third place, there is a change of emphasis in the way Jesus, the Christ, is presented in order to emphasise his humanity rather than his maleness. These three areas of change and development are of course linked; but, it will make for easier explanation if we look at them separately.

Patriarchy

We are all familiar with the name of "patriarch" used of the "fathers" of the Israelite people—Abraham, Isaac, and Jacob. These men were heads of their tribe/clan/family. It was the rule in ancient near-eastern society that the man was the head of the woman, who was the homemaker and mother of his children. In modern terms women then had few human rights, for they were regarded, in legal terms, as the possession of either their father or their husband. Their children, the fruit of their wombs, belonged to their husbands. Of course they could have (and did have) great influence over men through the use of their intelligence, beauty, sexual attraction and cooking but such influence came and went and had no other foundation than the individual personality and circumstances. This organisation of society in which the men are the rulers and the women the ruled is known as patriarchy (= the rule of families by fathers).

In fact as we look over the history of the ancient near East (where Biblical history took place) and the history of Europe up to modern times (where the Christian Church has been an integral part of society), we find that patriarchy in one form or another has existed at all times and in all places. Certainly there have been occasional queens of countries (e.g. Mary Tudor and Elizabeth I of England) but this has not changed the general picture of home and society, city and nation, being ruled by men. Put in stark terms, there has been a domination of women by men throughout recorded history. To put it this way is only to express the state of affairs as viewed from outside. Women, it is claimed, on the inside of patriarchy know from long and bitter experience that this domination has penetrated every aspect of women's lives and experience to make them dependent upon men for everything and to diminish and demean their true humanity. Thus a long struggle by women assisted by some men (which still goes on) has been necessary to begin to shake off this domination. In modern times feminism has become an important expression of this rising of women from under the rule of men into freedom and equality.

Feminist Christians, and it is they who are the leaders in the struggle for women's ordination, believe that patriarchy, even where the fathers/men were compassionate, has always been evil. Their starting point is the text in Genesis 1:27. "God created human beings in his own image; in the image of God he created them; male and female he created them." For them this underpins and underlines the doctrine of human equality to which they are already committed. Men and women are equal, they say, and thus males are not to dominate females nor females dominate males. Therefore any form of patriarchal rule by men (even good men) is wrong; when exercised by sinful men it is positively evil and oppressive of women.

Now the Old Testament on a plain reading appears to present God (to state the minimum) as mildly supportive of patriarchy. For the descriptions of Israelite and Jewish society in the Books of Moses, the historical books and even the Psalms and Prophets appear to take for granted that, under

God, men are to be the heads of families and society, with women as the obedient and submissive helpers. Further, only men could be priests in the temple and official teachers of the Law: there was no place for women in official religion and they had very few rights in Jewish law. Because of all this the feminist Christian feels obliged, on the basis of the conviction that total equality is God's will, to claim that there was a major misunderstanding of God's will by the men and women of Israel or, worse, a terrible rejection of God's will by the men of the tribes of Israel. If there had not been such a misunderstanding/rejection of the divine plan, then women would have been far more prominent in the pages of the Bible and there would have been more feminine titles for the Godhead in the prayers and worship of the Jews.

Of course, it is admitted that the Old Testament is not a complete disaster. There were bright spots in the history of Israel where women were allowed to function freely – e.g. there is Deborah who led the tribes in battle (Judges 4) and Ruth who has a whole book named after her. However the general picture is one of male dominance and female submission. Often the women were not aware of their position of submission and domination by men because they had never experienced anything other than this sad state of affairs. Thus the Old Testament cannot be called the Word of God as it stands. In fact, it is naive to call it so: yet it is valuable in many ways for its unique religious and moral insights. As long as the reader realises that it is essentially a collection of books written by men, who enjoyed domination in society at the time they had their experience of God, then she or he will not be led to conclude that its commendation of patriarchy is to be taken as the will of God for us today.

Feminists accept that the New Testament has a good number of examples, insights and doctrines which they believe support that equality which God intends for human society. They still insist however that the general framework of the message of Jesus and the teaching and practice of the early Church are that of patriarchy. They point out that the best N.T. scholars have shown that Jesus himself did not set out to remove patriarchy only to reform it and in this approach he was followed by the apostles. This reformist rather than destructive approach of Jesus explains what seems to be two opposite strands in the Gospels and Epistles. There are rejections of typical Jewish patriarchy – e.g. when Jesus calls women as disciples and allows them to minister to his needs, as he teaches the woman of Samaria by the well, and as he appears in his resurrected, immortalised body to the women before the men. There are further rejections of typical patriarchy when the apostle Paul compares the marriage of husband and wife to the marriage of Christ and his Church. "Husbands love your wives as Christ loved the Church and gave himself up for it. . ." (Ephesians 5:25). However, on the other hand, there are examples not only of the acceptance of patriarchy as the norm but also as in accord with the will of God. For example, when Paul tells women to be silent in church and to be taught at home by their husbands (1 Corinthians 14) and when he also tells slaves to be obedient to their masters (Colossians 3:18ff).

Further, feminists point out that Jesus gave a new lease of life to patriarchy by his constant addressing of God in heaven as "Abba [FATHER]". Only someone who thought in terms of the dominance and rule of fathers (even if they were compassionate men) could have expressed his unique relationship with God in terms of fatherhood and given as a model prayer the "Our Father. . . "! Further, they say that Paul made matters worse by referring to "the God and Father of our Lord Jesus Christ" and teaching the Gentile churches to pray to God as "Father". For, if people are to be taught to pray daily to "Our Father. . . " in the name of Jesus, the Lord, then they are going to think it right not only that men should dominate women but also appropriate and acceptable that women be second-class citizens in church and society at large.

Thus the New Testament like the Old Testament fails the test of commending without hesitation and without qualification equality for males and females. Therefore while it cannot be read and received as the actual written Word of God, it can nevertheless be seen to be a book in which there is much that is of great religious value. Here and there, there are great insights—such as that of Paul when he declares to the Galatians that in Christ there is perfect equality of male and female (3:28).

The net result of the judgement that patriarchy is evil is much more than the rejection of the traditional doctrine that the Bible is the written Word of God. It also means the rejection of such modern doctrines of the Bible as that associated with the name of Karl Barth – that the Bible is the written witness to the living Word of God (Jesus the Christ). Therefore everything in the Bible is open to question and ought to be tested to see whether or not it is supportive of the equality of the sexes and critical of the evils of patriarchy.

Because neither Jesus nor the apostles dealt a death blow to patriarchy and merely sought to reform it, they left open the possibility that their successors would allow the old style of patriarchy to return. And this is what happened, say the feminists. This is why there were no female clergy (presbyters or bishops) in the post-apostolic church and why eventually senior bishops came to be called "patriarchs" (e.g. in Jerusalem, Constantinople, Venice and Rome). Further the language used in the public Liturgy and in family prayers (addressing God as Father through Jesus the Lord) continued to commend the dominance of patriarchy in society at large. The Church merely reflected with minor modifications the evil patriarchy of Roman society. It did nothing for the cause of true equality of the sexes and never even so much as considered the ordination of women.

Language

The dominance of men over women is reflected in everyday language, the feminists maintain. On first appearance they seem to have a good point. They often cite the generic use of "man/men" to mean "human being(s)". Further, we are all familiar with the attempts to change such words as "chairman" into "chair" or "chairperson" in order to try to lose the masculinity implied by "chairman".

In the Church of England the Liturgical Commission under pressure from the feminist lobby has produced a report entitled *Making Women Visible* (1989) which attempts the task of removing from the newest prayer book of the Church, the *Alternative Service Book* (1980), what (from a feminist viewpoint) is called "excluding language". It is now common to hear Christian women say that they feel excluded from the liturgy of the Church of which they are members because that liturgy proceeds as if there were only men in the congregation. They complain that entering into the traditional language of prayer, however nourishing it may be in other ways, as women they experience themselves as absent, invisible, anomalous and even alien. So they have to make a continuous translation into inclusive language of the language which is male- oriented. Thus it is not surprising that they claim that this is distracting. Worse still, being surrounded by excluding language, they feel rejected in the very place where they seek acceptance at the deepest level of their beings.

The Commission had to be receptive to such cries from the heart of women, and it worked hard to show how offending words and phrases could be removed and replaced by non-exclusive or inclusive words and phrases. Thus much space is taken within the booklet with lists of changes. Its work got a mixed response in the General Synod and in reviews partly because the subject is exceedingly complex and cannot be reduced to the simple "either/or" of some feminist propaganda. For, even if it were possible to eradicate all so-called generic, sexist and excluding language from church services, there still remains the question as to whether the resulting, non-excluding language used would have any beauty or carry clear meaning. There is no guarantee either that making all these changes now will satisfy the feminist lobby or prove not to be out of date by the time they have been printed as options within prayer books.

The relationship between the use of non-exclusive (or inclusive) language for human beings and the ordination of women is straightforward. The use of exclusive/sexist language over the centuries, it is claimed, has served to help exclude women from being considered for priesthood and continues to do so today. When women are ordained however, the new state of affairs in the Church will need to be matched by a change in the language used of humanity. The renewed language must include the persons who are in fact presiding at the Eucharist. Women will certainly not want to say "who for us men and for our salvation came down from heaven" but rather "who for us and our salvation" or "who for human beings and their salvation".

There is a further dimension to the use of language. In worship we not only speak of humanity we also speak of and address the Godhead. Feminists are logical and they see that to achieve their goal of equality there must be changes in what they often now call "God-talk". Their argument is quite simple. The masculine (even macho) titles and names for God (e.g. "Lord", "King", "Father" and "Son") came into existence because men from within patriarchy thought of God in patriarchal terms. So it was natural that they chose to address God as if he were an infinite and eternal Lord and King of armies in heaven. And it was natural that Jesus should choose the word "Abba" (Aramaic for "Father") to convey his sense of oneness and yet submission to God in heaven. Because they see the origin of these names of God as arising from human experience within patriarchy, they judge that there is nothing particularly sacred about them. There is no reason, they believe, to keep on using them, especially when it is remembered that they actually serve to buttress the foundations of patriarchy in church, home and society. So they propose either that these be dropped completely or used sparingly along with feminine words such as "Mother" and "Sister" and with a full complement of such general non-excluding words for God as "Saviour, Sanctifier, Redeemer, Creator and Preserver".

The results of this call for inclusive language for the Godhead are beginning to make their impact on modern Anglican Liturgies. For example, in the Introduction to *A New Zealand Prayer Book* (1990) we are informed that: "the dialogue about inclusive language has now moved beyond merely referring to humanity. . . We have gradually been compelled in our pilgrimage to start searching for ways to address God in language which is other than masculine and triumphal. . . What we present is one fragile moment in the relentless on-going process of liturgical change." In the Introduction to the latest experimental services in the American Episcopal Church (in *Prayer Book Studies 30*) we are told that "many of the images used in the liturgy are 'masculine' and have been historically conditioned by the patriarchal nature not only of Jewish society but of much of Christian society. If we believe that this reflects cultural bias and is not part of the gospel, then the deliberate introduction of complementary 'feminine' images to our worship is desirable." This is the policy adopted in some of the new liturgies. Further, there is an alternative to the *Gloria Patri* which avoids masculine words.

 Honor and glory to the holy and undivided Trinity,
 God who creates, redeems and inspires;
 One in Three and Three in One,
 for ever and ever. Amen.

In avoiding "Father, Son and Holy Spirit", this form of words (we may note) also tends to depersonalise the Holy Trinity.

Thus the relationship between the ordination of women and inclusive language for the Godhead is easy to see, say the feminists. Over the centuries the describing and addressing of God as if he were a great macho, male, Father-King in the heavens has served to keep women in submission. Further, it has contributed to the doctrine that only the male can rightly represent the "eternal Male" in his heaven. However, when a woman is presiding at the Eucharist she does not have to address God as if she were living in a patriarchy. She can use expressions which recognise the feminine in the Godhead and which celebrate her own femininity.

Feminist Christians or supporters of feminism (who are of course both male and female) do not seem to be worried that changes in the naming and addressing of God will mean changes in our concepts and thus our doctrine of God. I think that they are so keen to win the battle for total equality of the sexes that they do not see that they are forcing doctrinal changes which include not only the setting aside of the Bible as the record of divine self-revelation but also the rejection of the received, classical doctrine of the Godhead as a Trinity of Persons.

The maleness of Jesus

Sometimes the impression is given by Christian feminists that they are a little embarrassed that the eternal Word, the Second Person of the Holy Trinity, became a human being as a male. They wish to set aside the traditional teaching that the maleness of Jesus is a sacred sign. Therefore their general approach is to insist that what matters about Jesus is not that he is a male—for as Saviour and Redeemer he could have been female—but that he is human being. His maleness is thus put on the same level as the colour of his eyes and hair, his height and weight and his complexion. They insist that it was the Word made flesh, the Second Person of the Trinity as human being who saved mankind by his life, death and resurrection. The fact that he was a male only gave a particular style to the way he was the Saviour: it made no essential contribution as such. For, they insist, if his maleness is a primary feature of the humanity taken by the eternal Word then he is only really the Saviour of men. Since he is the Saviour of all it is as human being that he is to be seen and appreciated.

Further, some feminists invite us to reflect upon what is the essence of the Lord's Supper, Holy Communion. In a country where rice not bread is the staple diet, is it permissible to change the bread for rice? Is it legitimate for rice to become the sacred sign of the body of Jesus instead of the bread (since of course Jesus himself used bread not rice)? Does the essence of Holy Communion reside in the use of bread alone or can it be conveyed through rice? If it is the basic food in a culture which becomes the sign then to use rice is not only permissible but right. Thus it may be argued that the sacred sign in the Messiah, Jesus of Nazareth, is not his maleness but his humanity and thus either a male priest or a female priest may be his representative. Of course this kind of reasoning harmonises with the feminist claim that human beings as male and female are equal in nature and identity, their only real difference being their sexual function. And it also explains the reluctance of feminist Christians to address Jesus as "Lord" which they see as a very masculine term and an aspect of patriarchy.

Conclusion

Those who advocate these changes, and in part seek to implement them where possible, do so, of course, from the vantage point of having first known and accepted orthodoxy before moving on to novel ways and teaching. But many of those who follow them and begin their Christian experience within this novelty will not have the stabilising and solid rock of orthodoxy upon which to stand (and to which to cling!) as they engage in experimental worship and develop new doctrines. Who can tell therefore into what possible heresies and errors as well as morality the new generation with the novel teaching will be led by the powerful winds of contemporary culture?

For the total agenda, on which there appears the ordination of women as apparently (but not in reality) the major item, is formidable. It is a call for massive changes to be made in Christian liturgy, doctrine and practice. In fact the programme is not only radical it is revolutionary. If it were adopted in full the result would be a religion which had few marks of that historic and dynamic Faith which prays to "the Father" in the name of the "Son", our Lord Jesus Christ, and in the power of the Holy Spirit, the Comforter.

Chapter Three

An inescapable question

A tolerant and moderate person who is generally inclined to favour women priests will probably have been upset or disturbed by the last chapter. I say this because of my experience in sharing the content of feminist theology and the implications of feminist thinking with people in both private conversations and talks to groups. Often the reaction I get is something like this: "Surely we can have the ordination of women without changes in the way in which we address God. Even if what you have described is happening in North America (where everything is exaggerated!) and New Zealand (which is so small and so far away) we cannot believe it will happen here in Britain. Surely the leadership in the English Movement for the Ordination of Women is not as advanced as their American counterparts." I have to point out as gently as possible that British Christian feminists appear to be well advanced in the content of the agenda they are seeking to see completed in holy mother Church. This is easily seen by reading the articles, book reviews and books which, for example, Monica Furlong and Janet Morley have published in the last decade.

The future

In all honesty I do not know whether or not the Church of England will find itself in the mid 1990's with a growing number of parishes using inclusive language in liturgy both of humanity and of the Godhead, if women are ordained priests say in 1992/3. It seems to me that there are suggestions that things will move in this direction even within the Liturgical Commission's booklet, *Making Women Visible*. I refer specifically to the commendation of new Canticles intended as options and designed to incorporate the supposed feminine in deity into worship (pp. 56-61). But also I refer to the "Litany of New Birth" which begins: "O gracious God of life and birth. How you labour, how you suffer, to bring forth the new creation".

Further, if what happened in a rural parish far away from feminist headquarters in London is any indication of what is happening elsewhere then I really do have justifiable fears! In a special Mothers' Union service a visiting female deacon, chaplain to the diocesan Mothers Union, began her prayers by addressing God in this way, "O God, Father and Mother of us all..." And there was a bishop present! As far as I know she received no episcopal reprimand. She took her prayer I believe from a booklet produce by the Movement for the Ordination of Women and she obviously thought that the source guaranteed the orthodoxy.

Bearing this in mind, I think it is prudent for those who feel that, taking all things into account and attempting to be fair and just, ordaining women to the priesthood is probably right, ought to face this question: Is it possible at this time (the 1990s) and place (western society) for the Church of England and other Anglican Churches to ordain women as priests without being drawn into adopting, officially or unofficially, the whole programme/agenda of which ordination is only one part? From what I have seen in my frequent visits to North America and from what I have gleaned from my survey of literature produced by those advocating women priests, I must say in all sincerity that to my mind this is an inescapable question forced upon all Anglican Christians. It is so, I believe, because of the very powerful cultural context in which we live and worship which insists that equality must mean identity of vocation.

Only God knows (and is sure to know) the correct answer to this question! My own judgment is that there is a high probability that the Church which ordains women will be drawn into the use of inclusive language for deity and thereby into serious doctrinal errors. If this occurs the fault will not lie primarily with the majority of the women ordained as priests, many of whom do not wish to see major changes in the way we address God in worship. Rather, it will lie with those who have pushed the adoption of inclusive language for humanity and deity, and also with those who have done little or nothing to stop its adoption, because they wished to be tolerant and kind. As far as the Church of England is concerned the responsibility will rest with the House of Bishops. This is why it is they who ought to face this question in an honest and open way.

I need now to explain why I think that there is a high probability of these changes occurring within a decade. The best way I can do it (without introducing a lot of new material into my presentation) is to seek to show that the whole tendency of the arguments given for women's ordination in chapter one is towards the total Christian feminist position. In fact, to show that because the general internal movement of the arguments is towards the total agenda of Christian feminism, they have therefore an inbuilt tendency within our present secular culture to serve that programme. Further, that they will introduce the whole programme unless there is a determined effort to reject and stop them immediately. I shall divide the ten reasons or arguments into several types and comment on each type.

Arguments from equality

The full equality of males and females is the aim of feminists. This is why they are vehemently opposed to all forms of patriarchy and paternalism of which they believe the Church is the last stronghold and bastion. When Betty Friedan, author of *The Feminist Mystique* (1963), was asked at an early stage in the feminist movement what she thought would be the most important effect of feminism, her reply was that it would be theological.

At least five [1,2,3,7,10] of the arguments appear either to arise from within or point to the feminist call for full equality of women in society and church. For example, the insistence that a woman has a right to have her call to the priesthood tested by the church authorities, is in essence a religious form of the claim to equal rights in all spheres of life. In fact it is a very subtle argument for no-one can say that she has no inner call since only God himself in the last resort knows whether or not she has a genuine call.

Then, with respect to the arguments based on the Pauline teaching that in Christ the distinction between male and female is removed and on the Genesis doctrine that both female and male are made in the image of God, it may be said that in and of themselves these texts (in Galatians and Genesis) do not naturally point to women's ordination. It is only in looking for texts to support that ordination that equality of male and female in both nature and identity/function is read out of these texts. They can just as well be read to imply equality of nature but not of identity (that is women are equal before God as human begins but this does not require an identical vocation to that of men). In other words the theme of equality in terms of identical calling appears to have been first in the mind and then read into the texts.

Arguments from a false view of ordained ministry

The bishop and the presbyter/priest are called by God to be Christ's servant and ambassador within the churches. The ordained minister is asked to represent Jesus Christ, Head of the Church, while being his servant and ambassador. In the ordination services of the Church of England found in the Ordinals of the *Book of Common Prayer* (1662) and the *Alternative Service Book* (1980) the ordained ministry is not described as representing human beings or the churches before and to God; but, rather, of representing Jesus Christ who is in heaven amongst and to human beings and the churches which are on earth. (It is true that in the Liturgy the priest does represent the congregation in that he prays on their behalf. However, the priest's representative relation to Christ is in every way prior to his relation to the church as its liturgical agent.)

The sixth and seventh arguments are based on the general notion that a presbyter/priest both represents human beings before God and represents the church to those human beings who are not of the church. Since human beings are male and female then (it is said) it is logical that priests ought to be male and female also. Therefore we see that this argument from the role of representing humanity is based on a view of the nature of the ordained ministry which is not taught by the official Anglican *Ordinals*, and which is very much a secondary and derived role of representation. It may be claimed with some justice therefore, that the source of this idea of male and female being required properly to represent humanity before God is the secular teaching of equality and equal rights for males and females. It is not derived from either the New Testament or the Ordinals. [We return to this important theme of representation in both chapter four and chapter six in the discussions of the priesthood and the maleness of Jesus.]

Turning to the ninth argument based on the *Articles of Religion* we note that it proceeds on the assumption that there is no major doctrinal change involved in ordaining women as priests. It is presumed that whether or not women are priests is a matter of the same order of importance as what vestments are required to be worn or what type of services are allowed/required. Thus a National Church has the power to go its own way on ordination as in other supposedly non-doctrinal matters. Here the argument about the rights of a National Church is historically sound but the claim that making women priests is only a matter of good order and not of doctrine is false.

Arguments based on a sound principle

The fourth argument rightly insists that Jesus gave to women a dignity and opportunity which were not there in official Judaism. This aspect of his liberating ministry has been brought out in recent years by a stream of erudite books which reveal how Jesus did not follow the way of the rabbis in his treatment of women but in certain respects treated women and men as equals in discipleship. However, we all know that while women were his disciples none were chosen as his apostles; and that while women worked with the apostles in a variety of missionary tasks and situations, none were appointed as presbyters or bishops in the new congregations in either the Jewish or non-Jewish world. So while the principle set forth is sound, the conclusion drawn from it that women should be presbyters now lacks firm foundation.

The eighth argument which is based on the unity of word and sacrament in the public Eucharist is, in my judgement, the soundest of all the ten arguments offered for women's ordination as priests. Having admitted women deacons to an official preaching ministry within Anglican Churches, the Bishops have (according to the principles set forth by the apostle Paul in 1 Corinthians 11 & 14 and 1 Timothy 2 & 3) committed to them that which in the Early Church belonged to the ministry of the pastor or presbyter or bishop of a congreation. In other words, though described as a deacon, the deacon has been admitted in function to that ministry which is peculiarly that of the presbyter or bishop in the New Testament. (The N. T. states nothing directly about the presidency of the Lord's Supper or Eucharist although the assumption is that the visiting apostle or the local senior pastor will preside at it.) The office of deacon was originally that of supervising and enabling Christ's ministry of compassion and social service in and through the congregation. Regrettably the modern deacon is so often but an apprentice presbyter/priest and the dimension of serving has virtually disappeared!

The argument from the development of doctrine

This has a particular interest for me because I published a book in the U.S.A. in 1978 entitled, *The Development of Doctrine in the Church*. The questions concerning what is a genuine development of doctrine, and how we can tell whether or not it is a genuine development, were brought into debate through John Henry Newman's *An Essay on the Development of Doctrine* (1845), written as he made the decision to leave the Church of England and join the Roman Catholic Church.

The claim that the ordination of women is a development of doctrine which the Church ought to make now, runs through most of the arguments for the ordination of women as priests. It is a view that is widely held. Certainly let us agree that where women are made priests and bishops there is an obvious development of doctrine. The question we need to face is: what kind of development is it? From daily experience we know that a development can be good or bad. We judge housing and commercial developments to be good or bad. Also we judge changes in policy by governments and companies as good or bad. We really cannot escape forming a judgement as to whether the change in doctrine brought into say the New Zealand Anglican Church by the ordaining there of women as priests and bishop is good or bad – that is good or bad for the sake of Jesus Christ, his truth, his gospel and his cause.

Classic examples of the development of doctrine in the history of the Church are the emergence of the doctrine of the Trinity (set forth in the Nicene-Constantinopolitan Creed of 381 and in the *Quicunque Vult* [Athanasian Creed]), of the Person of Christ (set forth in the Chalcedonian Definition of 451 and in the *Quicunque Vult*) and of Justification by faith alone by grace (in the Confessions of Faith of the Protestant Reformation). It is rightly claimed of these developments that they were/are both true to Scripture and also serve to illuminate Scripture when used as tools for interpretation of the Bible.

Is the doctrine of the ordination of women as priests and bishops clearly based upon sacred Scripture and does it harmonise with the rest of Christian doctrine as this has been believed, taught and confessed in the Churches? If it is and does then it can be called a genuine rather than a false development of doctrine.

A further consideration in this area is the context in which a development of doctrine occurs. I have to ask such questions as these. Should we expect a genuine development to occur in Churches which are getting smaller in numbers and engaged in little or no positive outreach, evangelism and expansion? Is God likely to be speaking clearly to Churches [e.g. the American Episcopal Church and the Church of England] which are contracting, showing many signs of being weak in faith, hope and charity and obviously suffering from the effects of secularisation? Are not modern claims to be making a development of doctrine more likely to be informed by secular considerations than by those of biblical truth and holiness?

The answers I find myself giving to these questions cause me to conclude that the likelihood that Anglican churches are pioneering a development of doctrine concerning the ordained ministry for the whole Church is minimal. Further, it appears to me that the enthusiasm involved in the making of the claim that there is a true development being made with ordinations in North America, New Zealand and elsewhere in the Anglican Communion is generated not from theological reflections on scriptural foundations but rather from enthusiasm for equality of opportunity for women in the Church. What I think that the Lord is calling us to consider is the right relation of male and female in our modern society where there is a crisis of marriage/motherhood/fatherhood with all the attendant social problems caused by this crisis. Here we could profitably develop the doctrine of sexuality, marriage and motherhood/fatherhood.

Conclusion

Perhaps I have now said enough to open the reader's mind to the possibility that the tendency of most of the arguments for ordaining women to the priesthood is most probably towards the secular doctrine of equality. I now invite those who recognise that ordaining women may possibly become the open door through which there enters into God's Church a whole set of new and old errors and heresies, to give serious consideration to what is often disparagingly called "the traditionalist position".

This description is correct in so far as the tradition of the Church over two millennia is taken seriously. However, it is incorrect if it means looking only backwards in nostalgia. Those who are genuinely committed to the revelation of God recorded in sacred Scripture together with the living Tradition of the Church do not only look back into history. Before they look back to the experience of the Church in history they look up in faith and love to the living and reigning Lord Jesus in heaven: as they look back they also look forward in hope to the

Second Coming of the same Lord Jesus and the consummation of all things: and as they look in these three directions they also look around upon the world intent on loving the neighbour.

Chapter 4

Ministry and Priesthood

The best way I can introduce the dynamic, traditionalist position is with some comments and reflections upon the important New Testament concepts of ministry and priesthood. These will serve to give us a basis from which to engage in theological thinking about equality, ordination and patriarchy.

Ministry in and with Jesus

The first Christians deliberately chose the word *diakonia* (a word used of the service rendered by the waiter at the table or by the servant in the household) to refer to the practical nature and reality of the new life for which God the Father had chosen them, the Incarnate Son had redeemed them and the Holy Spirit was sanctifying them. The apostles could think of no better noun to describe themselves, engaged in the work of reconciling people to God, than *diakonos* (servant/deacon). So it is not surprising that *diakonia*, the service rendered in the name of and in imitation of the Lord Jesus, became the hallmark of genuine Christianity. For the eternal Son "laid no claim to equality with God, but made himself nothing, assuming the form of a slave" in order to provide salvation for sinners. The first Christians knew that they were called to take upon themselves the "yoke of Jesus" and learn from him for he was "gentle and humble hearted". They did not need telling that such an attitude runs contrary to the normal functioning of the sinful, human heart, mind and will; thus they were much aware that it is only ever attainable and possible to the extent that a Christian is filled with the Holy Spirit.

On the basis of the New Testament we may affirm that it is as true today as it was in the apostolic age that all Christians share in the one ministry or service *(diakonia)* of Jesus Christ which he offered to the Father as the Messiah and which he is still offering to the Father as our King, Priest and Prophet in heaven. From the moment of their baptism all believers, whatever their age, sex or social standing, are called and set apart for ministry or service in and with Jesus Christ to the glory of God the Father and in and by the power of the Holy Spirit. There is no higher calling for any person on earth than this–to be engaged in and to share in the one ministry of Jesus Christ in the world. Such is the unique nature of this ministry that it can be undertaken anywhere at any time without any restriction or hindrance. No human circumstance short of insanity, being in a coma or death itself can prevent the exercise of it.

This means that as a Christian I can and ought to minister whatever my position in life. In the apostolic age the Christian slave was able to be a perfect minister of the Gospel in and with Jesus by an attitude and action which breathed the love of God. But so also the Christian master and owner of slaves was able to engage wholly in the ministry or service of Jesus by words and behaviour which brought grace and goodness into human relationships. Paul makes this very clear in his Epistles (see e.g. Colossians 3:22ff). Today it is not only the Christian in western society who is free to go here and there and enter this or that profession who can minister for God the Father in and with Jesus. The person unjustly imprisoned, the woman tied to her home as a mother and homemaker, the man working in drudgery on a production line, and the person lying in a hospital bed are all able and called in the power of the Holy Spirit to engage in the one ministry of Christ. Jesus Christ, exalted in heaven, is present throughout God's world in and through the Holy Spirit ministering by means of the willing hearts and hands of true Christians, and through them making present his reconciling and healing grace. If only each of us could truly believe this we could accept the deprivation and drudgeries of life as opportunities to minister in and with Jesus. Certainly it is easier said than done but such is the high and precious calling of God in Christ Jesus our Saviour.

But, it will be asked, what about "ministers of religion"—pastors of congregations, parish priests and diocesan bishops? I believe that the relationship of ministry I have been describing (which by the Spirit is in and with Christ) and particular offices in the Church is clear. At a basic level it may be said that every Christian has a vocation or calling from God to serve him in the sphere, responsibilities and jobs of life into which God has placed her/him. This is so whether that calling is to an office in the church or a regular job in the world. Thus a man may be called to be both a father and an engineer; a woman may be called to be a mother and a teacher. Likewise a woman may be called to be a mother and a deaconess and a man may be called to be a father and a pastor.

The vocation to be a pastor is a vocation to serve Christ in his Church by sharing in his specific care and teaching of his flock. The basic Christian calling to share in the general, serving ministry of Christ is united in a pastor with duty of oversight and leadership in a church. Thus those who are pastors and leaders in the Church are expected to reflect more intensely by their lives the basic and constant ministry of Christ in and through his Church and to the world. They are to be examples and encouragers of ministry to all the household of faith.

There is another way of expressing the connexion

between the basic ministry which is common to all Christians through baptism and the particular ministry of the offices of priest and bishop in the one, holy, catholic and apostolic Church. This is to see the historic ministry of the bishops (which they share with their priests) as continuing the ministry of the original Twelve apostles (and Paul). On this view (which is that of Orthodoxy, Roman Catholicism and parts of Anglicanism) the relationship with Christ as Head of the Church is emphasised so that there is a vital authority given to the ordained ministry to rule, to teach, to feed and to guide the Church – in love with humility.

The way we use words is often confusing. Within the Free Churches it is common to call the pastor "our minister" and to produce the impression that there is not a shared ministry of all members. Further, one specific office of ministry within the historic ordained ministry in the Church is called the diaconate and the one who exercises it is called a deacon (*diakonos*). Here again this word can suggest that others are not involved in diakonal service for our Lord. However, despite the problem with words the general concept is, I think, clear enough. The ordained pastor or bishop or presbyter or priest is to minister in such a way that he is the servant of the servants of God!

If we relate these biblical truths to the subject of this book then we can make certain claims straightaway. The first is this: that in a society where men are in positions of leadership and authority, a woman whose natural gifts and talents are under-used and whose natural freedom is curtailed, is not prevented in any way whatsoever by these adverse circumstances from exercising her basic Christian ministry. Though she is unable to enjoy and exercise her "full rights" as a person she is in no way restricted from thinking and acting in a Christlike way and thus exercising a full and complete ministry in and with Jesus, commending the reconciling love of God to fellow creatures, through loving example and word. In the second place within such a society a Christian man in the exercising of his headship/authority is obliged to exercise it as the head servant not as one who lords it over the woman. Only in such a way will he be truly engaged in Jesus' ministry. Other ways may seem appropriate, natural and acceptable but they will not be the ministry of the One who set aside his privileges and came not to be ministered unto but to minister and to give his life a ransom for many.

James I Packer has expressed the essence of what I am seeking to explain in this way:

"In all ministry, from the informal spontaneities of every member fellowship to the preaching, teaching, sacramental actions, and disciplinary pastoral care carried out by stated leaders, officially commissioned in the historic orders, Christ himself is the true minister, giving himself and his gifts to his needy people as they hear and share his word. That Christ is always the real minister is the deepest of all truths about ministry, yet it is one that is constantly forgotten, or at least disregarded. So what are we to do? The rational course is not far to seek. All structures of ministry in the church should be so designed as to create and sustain, with maximum force, faith-knowledge that it is Christ himself, Jesus of Nazareth risen and glorified, who ministers to us, communicating knowledge of his grace and goodness, his power and purpose, his will, work, and ways, making vivid to us his own reality, and drawing us deeper into his love for the Father and for the world; and doing all this through the words and acts of his ministering servants, who are his medium of ministry to us here and now" (*M.W.P.*, p.xii).

I cannot emphasise too strongly that this doctrine of Christ, the one and true Minister is fundamental for the whole doctrine of ministry and for what follows in this book.

A royal priesthood

As there is only one true Minister and his authentic ministry in which his people share, so there is only one true Priest and his gracious priesthood in which his people share. The Epistle to the Hebrews makes it clear that as Priest on earth Jesus offered himself at Calvary as the perfect and final atoning sacrifice for our sins: and having done so he was exalted to heaven in order to be our Priest there, to bring us with all our weaknesses to the Father for eternal life and divine blessings. He reigns at the Father's right hand in order to make intercession for us! Nowhere in the New Testament is any individual Christian called a priest. The word is reserved for the priests of the old covenant and of pagan temples. It is the Church as a whole which is a priestly body ministering constantly in Christ's name on the basis of what Christ has achieved as the Priest and is now doing as Priest.

In the Revelation of John we read these words of praise to the exalted Lord Jesus Christ: "To him who loves us and has set us free from our sins with his blood, who has made of us a royal house to serve as the priests of his God and Father–to him be glory and dominion for ever! Amen" (1:6). And we hear these words in a song of praise to Jesus, the Lamb of God: "You have made them a royal house of priests for our God" (5:10). Then Peter tells the members of the churches to whom he writes: "You form a holy priesthood to offer spiritual sacrifices acceptable to God through Jesus Christ" (1 Peter 2:5) and follows this with these powerful words: "You are a chosen race, a royal priesthood, a dedicated nation, a people claimed by God for his own to proclaim the glorious deeds of him who has called you out of darkness into his marvellous light" (2:9). On the basis of these texts we may happily speak of the royal priesthood of the whole Church of God. Priesthood here includes the privilege of a relationship and fellowship with God, but it also points to such duties as proclaiming the Gospel by word and deed and praying for humanity (1 Timothy 2:1). Further, Paul urges all Christians to "offer your very selves to God: a living sacrifice, dedicated and fit for his acceptance, the worship offered by mind and heart" (Romans 12:1). The royal priesthood expresses its priestly vocation by offering itself as a dedicated, committed life of serving the Lord Jesus Christ.

Here we face a problem. The New Testament does not use the singular "priest" to refer to any Christian at all; but, in the history of the Church one name for an ordained minister used from early times has been "priest". The quick answer to this problem is to say that "priest" stands for "presbyter" (in fact our English word "priest" is a medieval contraction of "presbyter"). Whether we use the word "presbyter" or "priest" one thing is clear: he does not function like a priest in the Temple of Jerusalem offering bloody sacrifices to God. Further the term "priesthood" is another word for the "presbyterate". Perhaps we need to be aware that the word "priest" has been preferred to "presbyter" because of the intimate association of this office with the celebration of Holy Communion and the belief that the presbyter is representing Christ, the High Priest, in his presiding at the service. Then in the Church of England the word "priest" has been used to distinguish the "presbyter" in the threefold ministry of bishop, presbyter/priest and deacon from the twofold ministry of Presbyterianism (presbyter and deacon).

The ministry of the presbyter/priest (who is inescapably a member of the one royal priesthood) is that of ruling, proclaiming the Word, and administering the Sacraments on behalf of Christ, the High Priest. The priest undertakes these activities in order to enable the whole body of the faithful to function for God as truly a royal priesthood. By his ordination his sharing in the royal priesthood is not increased; for that priesthood is the common possession of the whole Body of Christ. However, acting in Christ's name and place the bishop or priest has an unique union with Jesus, the High Priest. This union is separate from that common priesthood of all the people of God. In particular by what he is (an ordained man), says (proclaims the Gospel) and does (consecrates and distributes the bread and wine as the body and blood of Jesus) for and on behalf of the High Priest (who is also the heavenly Apostle, King and Prophet) in the Eucharist, the bishop or priest acts both as the representative and representation of Christ to the assembled body of the faithful. The whole congregation is then able by the Holy Spirit's action to act together as the royal priesthood and offer spiritual sacrifice to God in and through the Eucharist. It is important to note that the priest is not a priest because he is representing the congregation (as the royal priesthood) to God but because he is united in his office and ministry to Christ, the High Priest.

Graham Leonard, Bishop of London, has explained it in this way:

"By his calling of the Apostles and by his institution of the Eucharist, our Lord gave to his Church a structure by which it would be enabled to be sustained in its union with him, and witness to his unique High Priesthood. By his ordination, a man is set in a new relationship with Christ in his Body, the Church, with the particular role of being the sacramental sign of the fact that Christ is the Head of the Church and depends for its being and life upon the sacrifice of Christ. As celebrant of the eucharist, he is the instrument through whom the death and resurrection of Christ is shown forth. When he absolves the sinner he witnesses to the fact that it is Christ who forgives" (*M.W.P.*, p.19).

He also reminds us that the essential role of the ordained priest was beautifully expressed by the great poet, George Herbert, in his *A Priest to the Temple* where he said: "A priest is the deputy of Christ for the reducing of man to the obedience of Christ."

If we relate this biblical truth about the shared priesthood of all Christians to our specific task in this book, we can say, as we did with respect to ministry, that whatever our position in life, be it to live in freedom or in bondage, our participation in the royal priesthood does not increase or decrease. A woman living in patriarchy is able to share wholly in the priesthood of the faithful and a woman living in a society where there is total equality of women is likewise able to share wholly in this royal priesthood. The lack of civil rights in no way restricts the members of the royal priesthood from exercising their task of offering spiritual sacrifices to God in, with and through the great High Priest. Many members of the congregations whom St Peter described as the royal priesthood in his First Letter were slaves!

A right mental approach

In discussing the subject of ordination it is very important that we are aware of, and are rejoicing in, these fundamental truths which declare to our souls that all Christians share together in the one ministry and the one priesthood of the one Mediator between God and mankind, our Lord Jesus Christ, the unique Servant and High Priest. They make us aware that we are entering the sphere not of human rights and achievements but of the rich grace of God given to us in and through the death and resurrection of our Lord and Saviour Jesus Christ. Further, they encourage us to determine that in our explorations we ought to discipline our minds to bring them into harmony with our Christian calling in God's world of corporate sharing in Christ's continuing ministry and priesthood.

Then also we need to be aware and to affirm without any hesitation the equality of Christian men and women before God as those (i) who are made in his image and after his likeness and enjoy a common dignity; (ii) who enjoy equal and common fellowship in the body of Christ as they are being brought to full salvation by God; (iii) who are commissioned in their baptisms to fight together and with Christ against the world, flesh and devil; (iv) who as adopted children of the heavenly Father enjoy his blessings and communion with him and (v) as members of the royal priesthood and the one ministry of Christ serve God in worship and loving service each and every day.

Chapter 5

By whose authority?

Christian feminists wholeheartedly work for the ordination of women primarily because of the weight and authority of contemporary experience. It seems so obvious to them that modern views and insights on the equality of women are to be preferred to those of yesterday (be the "yesterday" that of the first part of the twentieth century or the apostolic age in the first century of the Christian era). Today whether we be feminists or not we must surely admit without hesitation and qualification that women have proved that they are capable of doing all the jobs and serving in all the professions which were normally done by/served in by men. Further, we can confidently look forward to more women, even those who also raise a family, taking their place on equal terms with men in all parts of the work-force.

However, let us be clear that the real issue or controversy over ordaining women is not about what women are doing and can do, or even about what women have achieved. It comes down to the question: Is it the will of God for his Church, of which Jesus Christ is the Head, that its ordained presbyters/priests and bishops be both male and female from now onwards? Since no-one apparently questions that God intends men to be in the ordained ministry – they have been priests and bishops now for nearly two millennia – the question becomes: Is it the will of God for his Church, of which Jesus Christ is the Head, that its ordained presbyters/priests and bishops from now onwards include women?

The authority of modern experience

Having set the question we now face the problem of where to look for the answer. It is possible to look immediately to modern culture and experience, as do the Christian feminists, and see there the answer proclaimed very clearly in terms of what women have achieved and are achieving. In theological terms this is then put in terms of God speaking to us in and through contemporary experience and insisting that this is (in certain circumstances) as valuable a source of knowledge of God's will as the pages of sacred Scripture or the wisdom of the saints in bygone centuries. Further, together with the claim that God's will is declared through the achievements of women this century goes the related claim that this is a genuine development of doctrine, moving the Church on from the positions held in the past into a new era of freedom and theology.

I have just put the argument from experience in the strong form as presented by feminists; but, it is more commonly encountered in a weaker form, which is held by many who would not wish to be called feminists. In this form, it is accepted and admitted that the knowledge of God's will is to be gained (as Anglicans have consistently affirmed since the sixteenth century) from the study of Scripture and Tradition using sanctified reason. However, the function of reason is extended from working only on the meaning of Scripture interpreted with the help and insights of the teaching of the Church in Creeds and Confessions of Faith [Tradition], to include the drawing of conclusions from reflecting upon contemporary experience in society. In fact Tradition itself is now often defined in such a way as to include our present experience in God's world and to urge us to discern what the Holy Spirit is saying to human beings within their contemporary experience.

Therefore, with this evaluation of Tradition, it is reasonable to "discern" from modern experience that women are equal in nature and identity to men (except in their sexual functions) and are thus rightful candidates for the ordained ministry. With this in mind it is possible then to return to Holy Scripture and Church History and look for indications there that the ordaining of women is God's will. Not a few of the books published in the last decade which argue (often in a gentle and attractive way) for the ordination of women as priests appear to have been written in this way. In other words (to use the American expression) the "mindset" is fixed before the study of Scripture and the historical teaching and experience of the Church is undertaken. Further, because the equality of women in society is a theme which we all accept (indeed a theme which we feel a moral obligation to accept) then our "mindset" or presupposition as we read and study the Bible has a powerful influence in all our thinking and reasoning.

Is there anything wrong with this approach in either the strong or the weak form? I would say that there is, because it tends to discount or to forget a fundamental and consistent theme in the Bible and Christian teaching over the centuries. This is that the world of culture, work and leisure is more often opposed to the perfect will of God than in harmony with it. While we are to give unto Caesar that which belongs to him and be exemplary citizens, we are also to give unto God that which belongs to him and be exemplary Christians. To be such we have to bear in mind that the apostle urges us to present ourselves to God as "a living sacrifice, dedicated and fit for his acceptance, the worship offered by mind and heart" and to "conform no longer to the pattern of this present world but be transformed by the renewal of [our] minds" for only "then you will be able to discern the will of God and to know what is good, acceptable and perfect" (Romans 12:1-2). The "present world" at its best is a long way from what God intended and what will be in "the new heaven and the new earth" of the age to come. Further, we cannot ignore the fact that in our baptism we are dedicated and ordained as members of Christ's army to fight against the world, the flesh and the devil. This surely stands as a warning to us that we are unlikely to know God's will from observing contemporary society alone for it is the very sphere where the world (humanity organised in such a way as to forget and disobey God), the flesh (human nature directed to selfish and ignoble ends) and Satan (the enemy of Christ and all baptized Christians) flourish and are encountered!

This is not to say that God does not and cannot speak to the listening ear through the ethos and events of modern society and culture. Prophets of Israel and prophets in the Christian Church have believed they discerned by God's inspiration a message from heaven in the events of history. Rather it is to insist that we are only capable of discerning God's will in contemporary movements after our minds have been informed and guided by that Revelation of God's will recorded in Sacred Scripture and received and experienced in the Church over many centuries. We need to remember that the Anglican formula of Scripture, tradition and reason begins with Scripture and not with unaided reason and so to the Bible we now turn.

The authority of Holy Scripture

Since the apostolic age and through every century the Church has believed, taught and confessed that the Bible is holy and set apart from all other books because it contains the record of the self-revelation of God to Israel, through Jesus Christ and his apostles. "The sacred writings have power to make you wise and lead you to salvation through faith in Christ Jesus" because "all inspired scripture has its use for teaching the truth and refuting error, or for reformation of manners and discipline in right living" (2 Timothy 3:15-16). These claims to the authority of the Bible in our beliefs about God, salvation, and the correct behaviour of disciples of Jesus Christ, have been consistently upheld by Greek/Russian Orthodoxy, Roman Catholicism and Protestantism. That is, the one, holy, catholic and apostolic Church has taught that what is Christian truth and error in fundamental matters cannot be known without careful study of the Bible, and the New Testament in particular.

Thus the "mind of Christ" has always been associated with that Truth to which the New Testament as a whole points and witnesses. Therefore to know the mind of Christ on any basic matter the Church has always turned first to the Bible in order to ascertain what is there taught and commended. At its best this method may be described as sitting at the feet of the Lord Jesus as listening and obedient disciples, meditating upon the New Testament in order to hear what he has to say in and through it by the Holy Spirit. The books of the Bible on their own and separated from the exalted Lord Jesus Christ and the Spirit who comes to us from the Father through the Son have nothing to tell us; but, read under the Lordship of the Son and by the illumination of the Spirit and to glorify the Father, these pages become to believing souls the living words of God.

Of course the Bible does not give direct and explicit guidance on all topics; yet it does lay down principles which can be applied to most if not all situations and problems. In the case of women, however, there is no doubt that the Church from the earliest to very recent days of the Christian era has believed, taught and confessed that the New Testament specifically forbids the ordination of women as presbyters/priests and bishops. (However, since Phoebe is called by Paul "a fellow-Christian who is a minister [literally "deacon"] in the church at Cenchreae" [Romans 16:1] and for other considerations there has always been the acceptance of the possibility of women deacons in the Church, even though that possibility has sometimes been remote.)

Orthodox, Roman Catholic and Protestant teachers have taken certain facts, indications and teaching in the New Testament as demonstrating that the mind and will of Jesus Christ is for an all-male ordained ministry to be pastors and shepherds of Christian congregations. Here are some of the passages of the New Testament in which they saw clearly the mind of Christ expressed.

(a) Jesus, the Master, chose only men to be his apostles (Mark 3:13-19), shared the Passover and first Lord's Supper with them (Mark 14:17-25) and gave to them his special commission to forgive sins in his name (John 20:19-23).

"Jesus appointed Twelve to be his companions and to be sent out to proclaim the Gospel, with authority to drive out demons." In Thursday of Holy Week "Jesus came in the evening to the house with the Twelve: during supper he took bread... took a cup." And on the evening of the first Easter Day Jesus came to them behind locked doors and "breathed on them, saying 'Receive the Holy Spirit! If you forgive anyone's sins they are forgiven...'"

(b) The apostles chose only men to be their pupils/assistants (2 Timothy 1:6) and the pastors [= elders or presbyters or bishops] of the newly-founded churches (Acts 20:17, 28; Philippians 1:1; 1 Timothy 3:1-7; 5:17-19; Titus 1:5-7; & 1 Peter 5:1-5).

Timothy was urged "to stir up the gift from God which was his through the laying on of" Paul's hands. The leaders from the church in Ephesus were told by Paul "to keep guard over yourselves and over all the flock of which the Holy Spirit has given you charge, as shepherds of the church of the Lord". In similar vein Peter appealed to the pastors in a large region (1 Peter 1:1) to "look after the flock of God whose shepherds you are" and to "do it not under compulsion but willingly as God would have it" done.

(c) The apostle Paul taught that in the Christian family the husband is the loving head of his wife (Ephesians 5:21ff) and in the local church women are not to exercise any ministry which places them in authority over men (1 Corinthians 14:33ff & 1 Timothy 2:11ff).

"Women must be subject to their husbands in everything" while husbands are "to love [their] wives as Christ loved the church and gave himself up for it". Further "as in all congregations of God's people, women should keep silent at the meeting" and "if there is something they want to know they can ask their husbands at home." This is because "their role is to learn, listening quietly and with due submission" for women are "not permitted to teach or dictate to the men".

All this seemed very clear to women and men throughout the history of the Church, and it may still seem clear, presented in this way, to some modern readers.

For many today, however, who have studied the New Testament in even a preliminary academic way it does not seem clear. This is because in most modern biblical commentaries on these passages, as well as in special studies of them, this traditional interpretation is challenged. It is also challenged in official church publications such as study-documents from the World Council of Churches and from the House of Bishops of the Church of England. In fact it is often set aside in favour of new interpretations (especially in academic literature) which cause these texts to lose their power as arguments for an all-male ordained ministry.

Two themes running through these modern interpretations are patriarchy and local circumstances/context. So, for example, it is said that Jesus chose men because that was the proper course of action in his day when patriarchy was the norm. The fact that he did so does not necessarily mean that in later times the Church is bound to a decision which belongs to a patriarchal society and culture. And, with respect to Paul's words to the churches he founded, it is argued that if the local circumstances are really understood, and other matters in the religious and social context are taken into consideration, it can be seen that Paul is only providing teaching for a specific, local situation which is not intended to be binding for all time and places.

Thus today we have to decide whether to follow that interpretation which has been held virtually everywhere and by all (until very recent times) or a modern one which claims that the old one is unscientific and produced by men (in sincerity) to support their own position. Certainly to accept one or other of the modern ones makes for an easy life in the modern church scene. This is because in our culture any statement that implies the inequality of women in terms of identity and vocation, or their submission even to the gentlest of men, is treated with amazement, even horror by a vocal minority.

At this stage it is important that I say what has often been said but needs to be emphasised. It is this. To hold that the clear teaching of Scripture and thus the mind and will of Christ is for an all-male ordained ministry of priest and bishop is not to declare that women are not equal to men. The same New Testament which [apparently] portrays a male headship in marriage and church also [clearly] insists that there is absolutely no discrimination whatsoever against women in terms of God's relationship with them as Creator to created and Redeemer to redeemed. How could there be so when the eternal Son took flesh and human nature in the womb of the Virgin Mary and was not ashamed to be known as her Son!

Women are baptised in the name of the Father, Son and Holy Spirit; the Holy Spirit as the Spirit of Christ regenerates them and comes to dwell in them; they are adopted by God into his family, the household of faith; by the blood of Christ they have access to the Father in prayer and spiritual fellowship and their prayers, trust, love and obedience are as acceptable to God as those of men; and they are called to be ministers each day through serving God in and through serving the neighbour and in proclaiming by word and deed the resurrection of Jesus from the dead. Men and women, both being made in the image of God and after his likeness, are equal before God in terms of relationship to the Godhead; but they are not identical for as two different sexes God has given to them in their equality different vocations and they are to complement one another. However, complementarity does not mean interchangeability.

Therefore we conclude that if there is a case for an all-male ordained ministry of priests and bishops (which we believe there is) it will and must rest firmly upon biblical foundations. All other possible foundations than the words of God-in-Christ (Matthew 7:24-27) will prove as sinking sand when the raging storms created by the world, the flesh and the devil assail them. Yet in the mercy and provision of God there are attached to these foundations the testimony and teaching of the Church over the centuries – Tradition.

Tradition

When the Lord Jesus ascended into heaven his disciples did not mourn and complain of his absence. Rather they rejoiced and waited for the gift of the Holy Spirit (the Paraclete, the Counsellor, the Comforter – see John 14-16) whom they knew would be in and with them always to mediate to them the presence and the mind of the exalted Lord Jesus. The same Spirit, whom Paul calls "the Spirit of Christ" (Romans 8), is given to and is present in the whole fellowship of baptised, believing Christians to lead them in worship and witness, faith and good works.

Therefore the Church of God is called both as a whole and in its manifestation as local congregations "the temple of the Holy Spirit": further the individual believer is described in the same way (1 Corinthians 3:16-17; 6:19). Led by the Spirit the Church of God throughout history has expressed its relationship to God the Father through Jesus Christ in a variety of ways—liturgies for all occasions, creeds and confessions of faith, hymns and music, symbols and signs (e.g. the sign of the cross), architecture and the plastic arts, sermons, books, evangelism, the founding of churches and monastic communities, works of mercy and social service and even from time to time the readiness to accept martyrdom for Christ's sake. Bearing this in mind we may say that Tradition occurs in the Church's proclamation of the Gospel, her liturgy, and the service she renders to God and the neighbour.

Because the Church is composed of sinners on their way to full salvation rather than of saints already totally saved, Tradition is never perfect and aspects of it can be and have been severely distorted through human frailty, error and sinfulness. This is why the well-known rule of St Vincent of Lérins (5th Cent.) has often been recalled and used to distinguish the vital and primary Tradition from secondary aspects and distorting accretions. The rule states that "in the Catholic Church one must see to it that we hold fast to that which was believed everywhere, always and by all; for that is catholic in the true and proper sense." If we use this rule with respect to the question of whether or not the ordination of women as priests is part of the Catholic Faith then there is absolutely no doubt as to what the answer is. The Catholic Faith is that only men, called by God, are to be appointed as priests and bishops in the Church.

The only way that this claim can be set aside is by proving beyond reasonable doubt that the Church has been so influenced by the [evil] patriarchal society, first of Palestine, then of the Mediterranean world, and finally of western Europe that the eyes and ears of all, (including the saints) have been closed to the promptings of the Lord Jesus Christ (through the Paraclete who indwells the Church and the individual soul) to open the door for women to be ordained. This is of course a tall order. If it is at all possible I suspect it will be easier to prove the case of the Church in the Middle Ages, when it had an apparently triumphalist mentality, than in the second and third centuries when the Church was often severely persecuted and when the blood of the martyrs was the seed of the Church.

I have noticed that a common theme in books advocating women's ordination is that the [supposed] insights of Jesus and the apostles pointing towards the total equality of women in the Church were quickly lost by the Early Church in the second and third centuries. The reasons given are that the social pressure of a patriarchal society, and the desire to conform to it overwhelmed the will to follow the lead that Jesus had set in his words and deeds. To me this is puzzling because the Church which was ready in that period to be persecuted, and to provide martyrs for the sake of Jesus and his Gospel, would surely have been ready to stand over against the patriarchal society of that time and give to women the opportunity to be presbyters (priests) in the congregations of Christ's flock, if it believed that such was the will and mind of Jesus Christ!

In claiming that Tradition speaks with one voice to confirm what Holy Scripture specifically teaches, I am not however claiming that everything which theologians and bishops have said about women is to be received and believed. Thomas Aquinas, the great theologian of the Middle Ages, for example, seemed to think that women were inferior in nature to men. "The male is more perfect in reason and stronger in virtue" than woman: and "woman is subject to man because of her weakness of nature both in spiritual vigour and in bodily strength." Other theologians spoke of the imperfection of the female mind! Such views are false accretions to the living Tradition which derive from Roman law and its legacy. They can and must be thrown away and forgotten, leaving behind the central teaching.

Finally, I hope it is now clear why the claim is made [both by those who oppose and even some of those who would like to see the ordination of women as priests] that the Church of England and the Anglican Communion should not even plan to ordain women as priests until a General Council of the Church (involving the Orthodox, Roman

Catholic, Anglican and such other Churches as may send members) has met to study, debate and come to a common mind on this matter.

Conclusion

Having reviewed the evidence we are therefore forced to the conclusion that any reasoned study of the New Testament and of Tradition serves only to support the arguments of those who are opposed to the ordination of women as priests. The apostolic and post-apostolic Church believed that the Lord Jesus Christ intended only men should be pastors of his flock, and we today should not act contrary to this. By the use of the same reason the conclusion is also reached that where the weight of contemporary wisdom stands in opposition to the teaching of Scripture and Tradition, the Church must go with the latter rather than the former. However powerful may be the attraction and influence of modern culture and however skilful people are in presenting social, secular and pragmatic reasons justifying a change in the doctrine and practice of the Church, the testimony of Scripture and Tradition will not go away, will not be neutralised and must be taken into account and followed.

Chapter 6

Affirming the masculine

Since the judgement that patriarchy is either a distortion or an evil is a vital, basic belief of most of those who argue for the ordination of women, it is important that we look at "male domination" in society and home and ask what is the will of God for the relationship of men and women. Together with reflections upon patriarchy and the divine will we shall also look at two other topics which are inter-related – the maleness of Jesus and the language we use in addressing God.

In the last chapter we placed ourselves under the authority of God-in-Christ, who speaks to us in and through sacred Scripture. Here, therefore, we must attempt to come to its pages as those who truly believe that its words were inspired by the Holy Spirit and that the same words by the same Spirit's illumination become for us today the words through which God addresses us concerning his will. We approach the Bible believing that God has given us a Revelation and provided Reconciliation in and through Jesus Christ, the Incarnate Word. "When the appointed time came, God sent his Son, born of a woman, born under the law, to buy freedom for those who were under the law, in order that we might attain the status of sons": and "to prove that you are sons, God has sent into our hearts the Spirit of his Son, crying 'Abba, Father!' You are therefore no longer a slave but a son and if a son an heir by God's own act" (Galatians 4:4-6).

We approach the Bible not to speculate as to whether or not God could have revealed himself and reconciled us in a totally different way but to receive, meditate upon, consider and accept what God is saying to us. We read the Bible and study its message as listening, obedient and faithful disciples. Of course we do not cease to use our intelligence and reason but we come with that spirit captured in the sentence of St Anselm: "I believe in order that I may understand." We do not bring to the Bible the "wisdom of contemporary culture" and dismiss everything therein which does not agree with it: but we seek to come to God in humility and teachability recognising that God reveals the secrets of his grace not to the "learned and wise but to the simple" (Luke 10:21-22).

Patriarchy

The question before us is not whether the society depicted in the Old Testament or the family life commended in the New Testament are patriarchal. Let us agree that they are so. Rather the question is whether in essence or nature they were evil, social structures. It is my contention that in principle patriarchy is the expression of God's will for the family because the contents of Scripture witness to this truth. This position (which has been that of the Christian Church through the centuries) may be put in simple form as follows:

1. God as Creator has made, and still makes, human beings in his image and after his likeness. There is, therefore, a fundamental equality of nature between male and female, and they share a common dignity. However, they are two different sexes (most obvious in their sexual organs and physical shape) and their equality is expressed in that they complement one another and have equal access to God for fellowship and in prayer.

2. God as Creator wills that in the relationship of male and female the man is given the position of headship and authority. However, this is a rule of love not of caprice; it brings greater responsibility and thus accountability to God as Judge. In turn the cooperation of the woman is offered willingly, not reluctantly, for it is part of her service to her Creator.

3. Because of human sin the image of God in which male and female are created is distorted and marred. Thus there is in the male a tendency to use his authority for selfish ends; human history is filled with examples of wicked treatment of women by men: and there is in the female a tendency to rebel against her secondary position and reject the authority of the husband or father.

4. Jesus accepted the fundamental equality of male and female and he emphasised that each had equal access to the Father in his name. A woman did not have to approach God through her husband's mediation for Jesus himself is for men and women "the Way, Truth and Life". Yet he did not set aside patriarchy: rather by his radical, ethical teaching he recalled people to what God originally intended for the relationship of male and female and promised the gift of salvation and the Spirit to guide and assist men and women to live according to God's perfect will. Because the greatest of all is the servant of all, the headship of the male was for Jesus the position of head-servant rather than oppressive master! Jesus, the Master, washed the disciples' sweaty feet—the work of a servant or slave.

5. Paul followed the teaching of Jesus and provided Christians with the model of Christ's marriage to his Church as that which they ought to follow: "Husbands, love your wives, as Christ loved the church and gave himself up for it to consecrate and cleanse it by water and word so that he might present the church to himself all glorious, with no

spot or wrinkle or anything of the sort, but holy and without blemish. In the same way men ought to love their wives as they love their own bodies" (Ephesians 5:25ff). The wife who is loved by a husband with the quality of love with which Christ loved/loves his Church will surely be happy to accept him as head.

6. Jesus and his apostles by their teaching and example made it clear that in the household of faith and the family of God the man is also to be in a position of leadership, headship and authority. Again, this is the position of being the servant of the servants of God rather than the dictatorial ruler of the faithful. Further, this does not prohibit the ministries of women within the congregation and from the congregation to the world: rather it sets them in a context of gracious headship and supervision (see chapter 7).

Understood in this sense, patriarchy is still viable within family and church life today and, moreover, is the will of God. If the contemporary church sets it aside preferring to follow the wisdom of contemporary culture then the church is disobeying its Lord and cannot expect his full blessing.

The maleness of Jesus

"Jesus" is the Greek form of "Joshua" and as such is a man's name. Though a few want to suggest that Jesus was not a male but an androgyne (a human being who is equally female and male) there is general agreement that Jesus was really and truly a male human being. So the question we have to face is this: is there any religious significance in the fact that Jesus was a male? Or we may want to face this question: Was it vital for our salvation that the eternal Word, the Second Person of the Holy Trinity, become human being as a male?

It is, I think, in general true to say that many of those who advocate the ordination of women as priests insist that there is no religious significance in the fact that the Incarnate Word became a male human being. In fact some go so far as to claim that the Word could have become incarnate as a woman and they point to the well-known female "Christa" upon the cross, as dramatically portraying this possibility.

Here I want to suggest first of all that the maleness of Jesus is entirely appropriate for the vocation of the Messiah, which the Word made flesh received from God the Father.

The following considerations point, I believe, to this appropriateness:

1. Since God as Creator gives to the male the position of head servant in the relationship of man and woman and in the family, the Messiah (= God's Anointed One) as the Head of the people of the new covenant needed to be a male.

2. All the prophecies of the Old Testament which look towards, or point to, the arrival of the Messiah presume that the Anointed One will be male.

3. The Mosaic priesthood, whose functions Jesus fulfilled and then made redundant, was a male priesthood and to fulfil it Jesus needed to be male. Further that priesthood of Melchizedek into which he entered and which he retains is also the priesthood of a male (see for details on this point the Epistle to the Hebrews).

4. In revealing to us what names we are to use in addressing and describing Godhead, he has given us the three names of Father, Son and Holy Spirit. Since the second person is the One who is Incarnate it is fitting that, as the eternal Son, he became human as a male.

Having commented upon the appropriateness of the male Messiah I must now relate that maleness to the sexuality of the priest and bishop. One argument for the ordination of women is that women can represent Christ as well and as adequately as can men. In this connexion the point is often made that the priest is not to be thought of as a representation but a representative of Christ. Thus it is said that even as a woman can represent a man and a man a woman (e.g. a male ambassador representing the Queen of England and a female ambassador representing a male President), so it is argued a woman can represent Christ, even though she cannot be a representation of him since he is male and she is female. Thus a woman may preach in his name and preside at the Eucharist in his name for there she is acting as representative and not representation of Christ.

The importance of this matter of representative/representation within the Church of England may be noted from the fact that it is the first issue singled out by the House of Bishops in their published report to the General Synod entitled, *The Ordination of Women to the Priesthood* (GS 829, 1988). They ask whether the function of representing Christ can be appropriately exercised by women as well as men and they have in mind the presidency of the Eucharist.

In response to the question, my first comment is that if the principle of headship of the man as head servant is previously accepted then this is a non-question for in the Liturgy the head servant will serve the servants of God by presiding over the proclamation of the Word and the administering of the Sacrament. The debate over representative and representation begins (in this context) only if there is doubt over the question of headship.

In the second place, I would like to say that if sexual correspondence is held to be required for truly representative ordained ministry the argument for an all-male presbyterate because of the maleness of Jesus Christ is compelling. The late C.S. Lewis argued that when a Church ordains a woman as a priest it becomes "less like a church" because its order then witnesses a degree less clearly to the spiritual reality which makes the Church, namely the gracious, lordly, saving ministry of Christ. In the army, Lewis wrote, "you salute the uniform not the wearer. Only one wearing the masculine uniform can (provisionally and till the Second Coming of Christ) represent the Lord to the Church; for we are all, corporately and individually, feminine to him." In the orders of both creation and redemption, what the man is to the woman is an emblem of what God is to all humanity: "we are dealing with male and female not merely as facts of nature but as live and awful shadows of realities utterly beyond our control and largely beyond our direct knowledge." Where our knowledge lacks fulness we ought not to innovate! (*Undeceptions*, 1971, pp.195-6)

Those members of the Church of England who look to both Orthodoxy and Roman Catholicism for doctrinal light in these circumstances note that there is a rich vein of theology in both to support the concept of representation. In Orthodox theology the bishop or priest is often presented as the icon or image of Christ and therefore it is insisted that the maleness of the priest is necessary for him genuinely to be an icon. This may seem rather an exaggerated claim to those who are unfamiliar with the place, meaning and function of icons in Orthodox worship. However, Elizabeth Behr-Siegel, a female theologian of Orthodoxy writes that in offering the Eucharist the bishop or priest "becomes... the icon of the Word Incarnate. It is this iconic character of the figure of the priest in Orthodox worship that... embodies the strongest argument against the admission of women to the sacramental priesthood" (*M.W.P.* p.109).

Likewise in Roman Catholic theology there is a rich and long- standing teaching that the bishop or priest as he presides at the Eucharist is there to act *in persona Christi* (in the name and person of Christ) as *alter Christus* (acting for Christ). Underlying this doctrine is the belief that the priest is a sacramental person whose effectiveness to be such depends both upon the authority conferred by ordination to the priesthood and by the obvious nature of the sacramental sign (i.e. the priest himself as male). If the priest were a woman then the natural resemblance to Christ as male would be absent from the celebration of the Eucharist, where it is Jesus, the male Messiah, who is the true yet invisible President of the divine Feast.

Therefore it would seem that there is much religious significance in the maleness of the humanity of the Word Incarnate. On the one side it is in and through his maleness that Jesus is united to the reality of male headship as the Creator's plan, and to the prophecies of the Old Testament which looked for a male Messiah. Then, on the other side, the maleness of Jesus requires that the priest be also male in order to be a true sacramental sign of the One of whom he is both representative and representation (icon)—Jesus, the High Priest in heaven.

Addresing God in worship

All informed Christians believe that God as God,

or God as Yahweh or Jehovah (Exodus 3:13-15), transcends sexuality. Though Creator of the two sexes, God as the infinite, eternal, holy Deity is neither male nor female. However, the threefold name by which the One God in Trinity is made known in the New Testament is "Father, Son and Holy Spirit".

Until very recently this did not pose a problem for Christians. They accepted that the eternal God is neither male nor female and they also accepted that this God is to be named and addressed in primarily male terms—"Father, Son, King, and Lord". It was taken for granted that since these were the names used by Jesus Christ and his apostles then this is how God wished to be addressed. So a typical Christian prayer was addressed to the Father in the name of the Son and by the power of the Holy Spirit. Converts were baptized in and the Blessing was given in the same threefold Name of the One God.

Of course there are many descriptions of God in the Bible (as a quick reading through the Psalter will show) and amongst these are some which are similes drawn from the experience of mother birds and women. So God is likened to the protective mother bird (Isaiah 31:5), the mother eagle (Deuteronomy 32:11), the midwife (Psalm 22:9), the nurse (Number 11:12), the mother who conceives (Numbers 11:12), the pregnant mother (Isaiah 46:3; 49:15), the mother giving birth (Isaiah 42:14), the mother who suckles (Isaiah 49:15), the mother who quietens (Psalm 131:2) and the mother who comforts (Isaiah 66:13). In this connexion we may also note that Jesus likened his own feelings to those of a mother bird: "O Jerusalem...how often have I longed to gather your children as a hen gathers her brood under her wings..." (Matthew 23:37).

To describe an aspect of God's care for his children is not the same as to address him. Jesus gave his disciples the model prayer "Our Father..." and in all the prayers recorded in the New Testament there is no indication that God is to be addressed other than by the names taught by Jesus and the apostles. Amongst these there is none which is feminine. Nowhere is there the slightest hint that we ought to address God as "Mother" or refer to the Godhead through the female pronoun "she". Therefore if we approach Scripture wanting to learn what God has to say to us then it is these masculine names of "Father, Son, King and Lord" that he will teach us to use when we address him in worship and prayer. Certainly this is how the Church has understood the Scriptures over the centuries.

Brian Wren, a hymn writer and a passionate advocate of addressing God through feminine as well as masculine names, has analysed several popular hymnbooks, the *Methodist Hymnbook* (London 1983) in particular. He has found that in them "the dominant metaphor system is KINGAFAP" by which he means "the King-God-Almighty-Father-Protector" (*What language shall I borrow?*, 1989, p.119). His intention is to try to change this system by including in worship a variety of female metaphors like mother, sister and midwife. He may succeed in some Free Churches but he has a big job with the major Churches because we find a similar pattern to his KINGAFAP in all the Liturgies of the Orthodox, Catholic and [most] Anglican Churches as well as in the ecumenical creeds. For example the Apostles' Creed begins, "I believe in God the Father Almighty..."

In and of themselves, and by themselves alone, it is true that these names of and for God can seem at times cold, forbidding and heavily masculine. However, their meaning is not established by the way they are used either by the popular media or in the history books or by individual imagination. It is established by the meaning poured into them by Jesus and his apostles against the background of the Old Testament. They are not to be seen as names for God arising only within human experience of God; but, rather, as names which, while having a reference-point in human experience, gather their meaning from the words of Jesus and the apostles.

Over the centuries theologians of the Church have been very much aware that such names as *Father, Son, Lord and King* when used of the Godhead are not being used as they are when they are used of human beings. So some have made use of what is known as the doctrine of analogy to seek to explain how these words function in discourse about and prayer to God. They explain that this is an analogy *sui generis* (of its own kind) – that is unique. It is not derived from the experience of human fatherhood but from God's own act of revelation in deed and in words.

God, as God, has established by his self-unveiling what is meant by Fatherhood. We must never forget that God was *Father* before he was Creator of the universe. As *Father* God did not create the *Son* and the *Holy Spirit*. The Son is eternally begotten of the Father and the Holy Spirit eternally proceeds from the Father and the Son. Therefore within the eternal holy love of the Blessed Trinity the Father eternally begets and the Son is begotten and the Holy Spirit eternally proceeds. Out of this eternity the Father created the universe (out of nothing) through his Word (Son) in and by the Holy Spirit. To ponder this for a while will hopefully make clear that to introduce the image of *Mother* alongside or to replace Father brings confusion into our attempts to think aright concerning both the eternity of the Godhead and the eternal relations of the Three Persons of the Holy Trinity. Thus we may go on to say that masculine symbolism for God points to the eternal movement of God, the Father, to the Son and Holy Spirit within the Holy Trinity, and thence to the world in initiative and creativity. In contrast feminine symbolism points to the movement of God returning to himself in the role of the Spirit within the Church which is responsive as the Bride of Christ.

In the last analysis the way we address God in

public worship will be determined by our doctrine of divine revelation and whether or not we accept the classic doctrine of the Trinity. If we see in Scripture the record of that revelation and thus look to it and the doctrine of the Trinity as arising in and from it as the basis of our faith and practice we will hesitate to call God by any other names than those he has made known.

Conclusion

Male domination is not the ministry or vocation to which God calls men. Rather he calls them to take their role of headship seriously as a duty unto himself and in loving service to others. This call is addressed both to fathers as heads of families and pastors as heads of the congregations of the family of God. Unless they do both family life and church life will be poorer because of this omission. God also calls women to cooperate with men to ensure that the will of God is expressed both in the family and in the church.

In that Jesus Christ revealed how the male can both lead all and be the servant of all there is nothing for women or men to be embarrassed about or ashamed of in genuine patriarchy! Further, in that God calls us to use masculine symbols in our naming of him, and in that he fills these with heavenly content and meaning, there is no need for women to be embarrassed to use them!

Chapter 7

Celebrating the feminine

My reader may well feel that on the basis of what I have presented in chapters five and six there is little or no place in the church for either the celebration of the feminine or the special vocations of women. Here I want to affirm that there is a full place for women's vocations in God's Church as well as the need and duty to celebrate the feminine.

Mary, mother of our Lord

If proof were needed that God genuinely loves women and calls them into his service then it is supplied by the ministry and vocation of Mary, the teenage virgin of Galilee. Let us take a moment to reflect upon Mary. She was chosen by God to become the mother of our Lord (who is the eternal Son of God Incarnate). She conceived his flesh/humanity in her womb, she gave birth to the baby Jesus, she fed him at her breasts and nurtured him, and she cared for him as his mother for thirty years before he began his public Ministry. Even then she continued to care for him and was there at the end, standing at the foot of his cross.

Her *yes* to God both at the beginning when the angel visited her and her continuing *yes* for the next thirty-three years remain before the church as a supreme example of faith and faithfulness. For she was both the God-bearer (*Theotokos*), a unique vocation, and the first disciple of her Son (thus the first Christian). Thus in the Liturgies of the Church over the centuries she is always named before the apostles: for by the grace and election of God she comes before the apostles and martyrs. The eternal Son became a male human being: to do so he needed the total cooperation, love and faith of a woman. Mary was that woman. No wonder Elizabeth on seeing the pregnant Mary was filled with the Holy Spirit and "exclaimed in a loud voice, 'God's blessing is on you above all women, and his blessing is on the fruit of your womb'" (Luke 1:42). The highest elevation of human nature took place in the masculine when the divine person of the Son of God became man and male; but, the highest elevation of the human person took place in the feminine, in Mary, the Virgin Mother of our Lord. To celebrate this position of Mary by the grace of

God the Byzantine liturgy sings that she is more exalted than the cherubim and more glorious that the seraphim. The greatest of all creatures after God himself is not an angel but a woman!

Though to do so is regarded by many as old-fashioned today, I believe that Christians cannot talk about the ministry of women without reflecting upon Mary's ministry and vocation. The fact that many Protestants have been hesitant and shy to do this, and some Roman Catholics have been over zealous in doing it, does not negate such reflection. First of all, in and by Mary we are able to gain a right way of thinking about the Church of God. A common cry today is that the Church is an oppressive organisation dominated by men for the sake of men. Yet the Church as seen in and through Mary (the first Christian and because Mother or our Lord also Mother of those who are united by faith with her to him) is not an *It* but a *She*. In fact to use the powerful metaphor used by Jesus and Paul the Church is nothing less than the Bride of Christ who is the heavenly Bridegroom.

In the second place, in and by Mary, we see that the response of the created order and in particular of the Church to God is to be a *feminine* response. She was totally receptive to the word of God addressed to her and the action of God upon and within her. As the *new Eve* she symbolised the created order whose proper calling is that of receiving God's grace and responding in grateful admiration and loving service. As the first disciple she symbolised the people of the new covenant and new creation whose proper calling is faith with faithfulness and service with joy. Thus while the names for God are masculine the response God calls for from both women and men is a feminine response - that of humble reception of his initiative of grace and ready and willing submission to his gracious and perfect will.

Thus we see that woman in the gracious plan of God is destined for something incomparably greater than the vocation of apostle or presbyter/priest. Only a man can be a priest (if he is fully to represent Christ as a sacramental sign) but only a woman can be and is *Theotokos* (the God-bearer), mother of our Lord. It is a woman, not a man, who represents the whole of humanity in saying a joyful "Yes" to the coming of God in the flesh, the arrival of the eternal Word incarnate. It is a woman not a man who is the supreme model and embodiment of the church as Bride and Mother of believers. And it is femininity rather than masculinity which symbolizes the right attitude of the whole person before God. To these thoughts we may add these words from a lecture by John Saward:

"There is a kind of poverty about the male which Christ puts to use in ordination. The man's role in generation is outside himself, in the womb of the woman, and in utter dependence upon the power of God. Woman, by contrast, receives and then retains and nourishes the gift of life within herself. Similarly, men image Christ in the priesthood, but they are not Christ. Their inadequacy is shown up by the greatness of the part they play. By contrast, women symbolize creation and at the same time are creatures. In other words, women embody the very values they symbolize. Men do no more than point."

Though we may want to argue that the woman's role in conception is more than John Saward allows, his main point is clear and stands. Thus we may say that the Church as a whole is Marian, truly feminine, open and ready to receive the energising life and dynamic truth of her Life-giver and Head: yet the male ordained ministry is just one part of the Church, with the humble vocation to serve the (feminine) whole.

Women as disciples and missionaries

It is not surprising to those who read the whole of the Gospels, noting our Lord's clear affirmation of the dignity of women and their profound faith in him that it is the women who are at the cross of Jesus while all the male disciples except one have deserted him. Women were first to enter the empty tomb. Women were first to embrace the pierced feet of the Risen Lord and were indeed the first witnesses and ambassadors of the resurrection. It is they who told the apostles that Jesus has risen from the dead and truly alive.

Each Good Friday and Easter Day as we read and meditate upon the final part of the four Gospels, I find myself deeply impressed by the faith and grace evident in those women who stood by Jesus to the painful end and who two days later went to his tomb to be with him and to reveal their love for him. How our Lord must have loved his female disciples, I say to myself, by choosing to show himself as the resurrected Lord of glory first of all to them!

Though our Lord did not choose a woman as an apostle, he did include women as recipients of the Holy Spirit whom he sent from the Father. They were amongst the assembled disciples on the Day of Pentecost after his Ascension into heaven (Acts 2) and with the men were filled with the Holy Spirit and endowed with spiritual gifts. Therefore, it is entirely to be expected that we find women sharing in the missionary task of the Church as that is described in the Acts of the Apostles and referred to in the Epistles. Luke provides what we may call five vignettes about Christian women. In the mother of John Mark (Acts 12:12-17) and in Lydia (Acts 16:40) we encounter women acting as "mothers" and "hostesses" for the young Christian churches in Jerusalem and Philippi. They provide a place to meet together with lodging and food. Tabitha (Acts 9:36ff) also served in this way but appears also to have had a particular ministry to widows—serving as a deaconess. The daughters of Philip (Acts 21:9) possessed the gift of prophecy and were possibly part of an order of ministry of single women within the apostolic churches. Finally there is the very important presentation of Priscilla (Acts 18:26) who is mentioned with her husband (a colleague in missionary work) in other places as well (Romans 16:3). She is a teacher who serves the Lord with her husband and who expounds the way of the Lord Jesus to enquirers, both men and women.

A careful reading of Romans 16 also reveals that Paul was not embarrassed but rather delighted to have not a few women engaged with him in the advance of the Gospel and the planting of churches throughout the Roman Empire. We may note Phoebe "a fellow-Christian who is a minister (*diakonos*) in the church at Cenchreae" (v.1). Then there is Priscilla whom we have met in the Acts of the Apostles and who Paul describes as "having risked her neck to save my life" (v.3). Mary is said to be "a hard worker" (v.6) while Junia (with her husband, Andronicus) was formerly a comrade of Paul's in captivity and "eminent among the apostles" (v.7). In other words Junia and her husband were a man and wife team engaged in evangelism and churchplanting ("apostle" here meaning "one who is sent on a mission", an itinerant missionary), and they had worked as such with Paul. Finally we may note the delightful duo of Tryphena and Tryphosa (v.12) who are said "to work hard in the Lord's service".

Though the vocation of women as missionaries for Jesus was accepted with gratitude, there is no record either in apostolic times or in the centuries immediately afterwards of a woman being set apart to serve a congregation as a presbyter or bishop. There seems to have been an understanding and acceptance that only men, called by Christ and empowered by his Spirit, were to fulfil these vocations of ruling "the household of faith".

Deacons and Nuns

In the period after the apostolic age women continued to live as faithful Christians and so what they had done in the first decades of Christianity they continued to do. Their homes were centres of fellowship, teaching and evangelism. They told of their love for Jesus and their salvation in him when they went to market and other public places and occasions. However, it seems to have been the case (the evidence is scanty) that they were less evident in public ministry (e.g. husband and wife teams of evangelists) as the years rolled by. However, we do know that there were orders of "widows", "virgins" and female "deacons" whose duties in the churches were specifically related to ministering to women through visiting and teaching, assisting at their baptisms and burials and so on. With the arrival of the monastic movement in the fourth century these orders for women gradually disappeared as women entered convents to serve God in and through the community life and outreach of these fellowships of dedicated women. We all know what a tremendous service convents of nuns have rendered to the Church and society in general through their intercessions and their loving service in teaching, nursing and spiritual counsel and other forms of ministry with and for Jesus. In the Middle Ages scholastic theologians, with their typical thoroughness, produced arguments for a male-only priesthood which may seem to us somewhat exaggerated and unnecessary, since at that time few women if any at all thought God was calling them into the order of priests or bishops.

With the arrival of the national Protestant Churches in the sixteenth century, and later of evangelical denominations such as Methodism, the situation of women in the congregations became not unlike that which we noticed in the Acts of the Apostles and in Romans 16. Though women were not pastors or involved in public preaching, they were there proclaiming the Gospel by using their homes as loving centres of faith and fellowship, evangelism and mission. Further some of them were able to join with their husbands to work as colleagues especially with children and deprived people. Then, of course, some women took to writing to produce literature whose aim was to explain and commend the Gospel of Jesus.

It was perhaps inevitable that within one or more of the many Protestant denominations that had come into existence by the nineteenth century a woman would be appointed as a pastor of a congregation. That wonderful woman, Catherine Booth, began to preach in public in 1860 alongside her husband, the first general of the Salvation Army. Soon afterwards the call of women to positions of leadership and to public preaching was formally recognised in the Salvation Army. But the more traditional Protestant denominations of Europe waited until after the Second World War to agree to go ahead with their first ordinations of women. By 1990 most of them, but not all, have women clergy serving congregations. It is important to recognise, however, that the setting apart of women as preachers and pastors in Free Churches did not arise directly from any secular feminist pressures. Rather, it was a sense of desiring to participate fully in the life of the Church and a knowledge that on "the foreign mission field" women had functioned in practice if not in name as pastors and presbyters. In contrast, the conservative denominations which have not allowed women to become pastors claim to be following the teachings of Paul (especially in 1 Timothy 2-3) and do not allow women to preach in the main service on the Lord's Day.

How does a person who believes that women, though equal before God in every respect, are not (according to his revealed will) to be pastors or presbyters or bishops explain the preaching and sacramental ministry of women which is apparently (obviously) so often blessed by our Lord? The answer is simple and is provided by James I Packer: "God has blessed his people before through intrinsically inappropriate arrangements and might be doing the same again" in the case of women pastors. For "the kindness of God in practice does not resolve matters of principle" (*M.W.P.* p.viii).

A way forward within Anglicanism

What is needed is the affirmation and practical realisation of the full participation in the every-member ministry of the congregations of the baptised by women as well as men. God has given to each Christian both natural and spiritual gifts and these are surely to be used for the edification of the whole body, the mission to the world, and to the glory of God. Unless this is clearly understood and accepted then there will be constant complaints that some women are deprived of "ministry to which they have a call". There are so many ways in which men and women, sharing in the one ministry of Christ, can actually minister these days—through music, visitation of homes, hospitals, old people's centres, in administration of affairs of the congregation, in caring for and instructing children and young people, in hospitality, in physical work for those who need help (e.g. the elderly living alone), in Bible study and prayer groups and in many other activities (which may be noticed in any active parish congregation). Then, of course, there is the ministry of prayer. This is a ministry which all can perform for we are encouraged by our Lord and the apostles to make intercessions for all people. It is easy to describe it but difficult to do it in practice.

The question, however, remains as to what forms of public ministry women can perform if they [along with the majority of men who do not receive Christ's call] are excluded by the will of the Lord Jesus from the office of presbyter/priest and bishop.

Obviously there is already open to them the office of deacon and the Church of England in 1990 has about 1200 female deacons. However, there is a difficulty here. This office has been devalued and distorted by becoming a kind of stepping stone to the presbyterate/priesthood. In the Anglican Communion it has been the custom to ordain the ordinand as deacon one year and as priest the next year. So the period as a deacon has become a kind of apprenticeship or probationary period waiting for the real thing – the ordination as priest. This office of deacon must be restored to a genuine office of public ministry in the Church so that women and men can enter it and do so with a sense of call and with a commitment to be deacons for life. Though there has been much talk about this restoration very little has been done about it. As long as a person who is a deacon thinks that he/she must move up the ladder to become a priest as soon as possible then the diaconate has little relevance as a public vocation and ministry in God's Church. Therefore before we can sort out appropriate forms of public ministry for women we need both to accept and practice an all-member ministry in our congregations and to create a diaconate which is a vocation for life and which has a real accepted content of duties and tasks (which do not include the presidency of the Eucharist and the public preaching of the Word).

In the Church of England, in particular, if there is a renewal of the diaconate, then there will have to be a major shake-up of the way in which the ordained ministry is understood, organised and financed. The work of the parish rector or vicar is seen as what a presbyter/priest actually does and this is the model which lies behind much of the debate about ordination. Then most of the money raised by the Church Commissioners, and given in collections in the parishes, goes to provide stipends for the support of incumbents (rectors and vicars) in individual parishes. Ways will have to be devised which fully utilise and reward financially on equal terms those female and male clergy who are permanent deacons or are in such other offices for women as may be devised and authorised. At the moment there is not equality in opportunity, standing or financial remuneration for women who have particular vocations within the official ministries of the Church.

I have no doubt that if we could give our whole attention to working out the public ministries into which our Lord is calling women today, instead of using our minds and energies to argue about equality of opportunity and identity, then we would quickly make progress in devising official ministries for women which could and would honour God, exalt Christ, and fulfil their vocations to work full-time within and for the Church. Such official ministries could start from those of deacon and nun by developing them as well as by adding to them others which specifically relate to the mission of the Church in the modern world.

Conclusion

By the grace of God the highest elevation of a human person took place in the feminine, in Mary, mother of our Lord. In her receptivity and faithfulness Mary symbolises for the whole Church (and creation) its proper response to God's initiative of grace. Thus the Church is truly the Bride of Christ in reality when she is responsive to the attention of the Bridegroom.

Women not only symbolise creation they also receive gifts of the Spirit in the new covenant for a rich variety of forms of ministry. Though they are not called to those public ministries which imply headship they are being called by our Lord to a variety of ways of serving him today: when the clamour to make it possible for them to be priests dies down we shall hear "what the Spirit is saying to the churches" concerning their public vocations in the Church.

Chapter 8

CONCLUSION

It is now possible in the context of what has been affirmed about the servant ministry and royal priesthood of all baptised believers in Jesus Christ, the Servant and the High Priest, to bring together the reasons why, I believe, this same Lord Jesus does not call women to the presbyterate/priesthood and episcopate today.

To clear the deck I must first emphasise that his exclusion of women from these offices is:

(a) not because women have an inferior status to men. They are equal in dignity and honour as God's creatures.

(b) not because women are emotionally, mentally and physically incapable of doing the tasks associated with the work of a presbyter or bishop. Obviously they are capable of these tasks.

(c) not because women are religiously "unclean"

through their monthly menstruation. Such ideas of uncleanness belong to the old not the new covenant.

(d) not because God loves women less than he does men. God loves male and female equally with an everlasting love.

The exclusion is for theological reasons—that is, they arise from within God's revelation which is recorded for us in the Old and New Testaments. I have already provided them in the context of my discussions in the last three chapters but here for the sake of clarity I shall set them out briefly.

1. *The witness of the New Testament*

While it is evident that women engaged in a variety of tasks in evangelism and planting of churches in and after the apostolic age, there is no hint in the New Testament that women were chosen as bishops or presbyters. Further the apostle Paul placed restrictions on what Christian women, in comparison with men, could do when the church met for corporate worship (see 1 Corinthians 11:2-16; 14:33-36; 1 Timothy 2:8-14). These restrictions were based on the doctrines of creation and the origin of sin in human life (the fall) as these are provided in Genesis and confirmed in the New Testament (see especially 1 Timothy 2:12-14).

2. *The testimony of Tradition*

In the Early Church two facts were taken at their face value:

(i) that Jesus had chosen only men as his inner core of disciples, the Twelve, and Paul as the apostle to the Gentiles;

(ii) that Paul had taught that women were not to preside over and preach in the worshipping congregations. Thus while women served as deacons there was no attempt to set them apart as presbyters. This position and approach remained constant in the whole Church (Orthodox, Catholic and Protestant) until very recently. Doubts that the New Testament restricts the presbyterate to men only arose with the beginnings of what we now call the feminist movement.

3. *The person and place of Jesus Christ*

Christianity affirms the dynamically central position of Jesus Christ, the exalted Lord, and the union of believers with him through the Holy Spirit. Jesus is the head, husband and cornerstone of the Church of God (Ephesians) and the royal messenger and high priest (Hebrews). To know God in and through Christ is to have eternal life and thus Christianity is in essence trusting, following, imitating, loving and serving this Lord Jesus. Therefore, as I have often emphasised, all genuine Christian ministry of the whole church is in and with him for it is his ministry.

However, Jesus, as the incarnate Son of God, was a male and so the Church has reasoned over the centuries that it is and will always be easier and more straightforward to remember that he is present and active in the congregation through the specific and ordained ministry of Word and Sacraments when his human agent is also a male. At its simplest level this is only to state that a male is best represented by another male. In its developed form it can be presented in terms of the priest as the icon of Christ (in Orthodoxy) or in terms of the priest in his sacramental activity sharing in a special way in Christ's high priesthood (in Roman Catholicism).

The maleness of Jesus is not accidental but essential to God's plan of redemption for the sinful human race. Jesus is the "Second Adam", the "Last Adam" and our "Prophet, Priest and King" and his maleness is essential to all these.

4. *The nature and reality of human beings*

God made human beings as male and female equal in dignity. His plan for their relationship is given in both Old and New Testaments as "the man to lead, the woman to support: man to initiate, woman to enable; man to take responsibility for the well being of women, women to take responsibility for helping men." Since presbyters and bishops are placed over the household of faith as pastors and leaders they cannot be women. For what God intended in creating the human race he intends as the rule in the society of those whom he is re-creating in the image of Jesus Christ.

5. The real character of the Church of God.

The Church of God is not in the world to be as the world. If it becomes as the world then it has ceased to be the salt of the world and the light of the world. The Church is not in the world to take its guidelines from the best (in its judgment) that society can offer. If it does this then it sets aside the sacred Scriptures as the rule of its faith and morality. The Church is not in the world to serve the world as the world thinks a religious organisation ought to serve (as a humanitarian society only).

The Church of God today is the continuation of the Church of yesterday and it will be the Church perfected and glorified tomorrow. It has a supernatural character because the Lord Jesus is present in it by his Spirit so that it is his Bride and his Body. Thus its ordained ministry does not exist to symbolise and express what the modern world regards as vitally important but rather to be and do what the Lord Jesus desires. His word tells us that he wants male presbyters and bishops.

6. The celebration of the feminine.

Mary was the first disciple of her Son and the first

Christian but she was not an apostle. She is a symbol for us of both the true position of a woman as God's creature and of the Church as the Bride of Christ. She was wholly receptive to the word of God addressed to her and the action of God upon her. She is the Mother of our Lord and our Mother (as we are in him) and she shows that women find their true ministry and vocation not in male roles of headship and representing (being an icon of) Christ but in their female role of receptivity, cooperation and response. From this perspective and in this spirit there are many possibilities for the public ministries of women in the Church of God, developing from the ancient and honourable vocations of deacon and nun.

★ ★ ★ ★ ★ ★ ★ ★ ★

I believe that these reasons for maintaining an all-male presbyterate or priesthood and episcopate do not point to male domination or male domineering. Rather they point to men, called by God and already wholly involved in the one ministry and priesthood of Christ, receiving from Christ particular responsibilities concerning the care and rule of the churches, the preaching and teaching of the Word and the administration of the Sacraments. If the men who are priests and bishops do not function as the servants of the servants of God then they are failing to live up to their sacred calling. They contribute to the call for the Church to follow the wisdom of the world!

I close this book by quoting from the *Report* of the House of Bishops (1988) of the Church of England. Here the minority of bishops who opposed the ordaining of women as priests speaks:

"There are those of us who believe that by continuing to ordain only men to the priesthood the Church of England will remain most faithful to the long tradition of the Church and continue to bear witness to the Gospel in our generation. An all male priesthood will witness to those things about the nature and being of God which were signified in the particularity of Jesus' maleness: a male priesthood will continue most faithfully to represent the priesthood of Christ in the sacramental life of the Church; it will point to the role and status of men in relation to women according to the purposes of God in creation and redemption, by testifying to the headship of men over women and the proper subordination of women to men. Those of us who hold this view believe this to be an important witness in our society as men and women struggle to find new patterns of relationships and new roles for women. Further, an all male priesthood will continue to be a powerful witness to the continuity of the Church's ministry from the time of the Apostles till today, and a link with the Roman Catholic, Eastern Orthodox and Old Catholic Churches, and thus be important for the continuity, the unity and the communion of the Church" (GS 829, p.98).

I hope that the diocesan synods and the General Synod of the Church of England, as well as other parts of the Anglican Communion, will take these words to heart.

Appendix

The proposed legislation for the C. of E.

In November 1989 the General Synod of the Chuch of England gave provisional approval to a Measure called "Priests (Ordination of Women) Measure" and referred it to the dioceses. Therefore during 1991 every diocesan synod (and probably every deanery synod and many parochial councils) will be discussing the Measure. It is important to note that they will not be discussing the general principle of the ordination of women to the priesthood but the present Measure as it stands for it cannot be amended.

In order to proceed this Measure must get a simple majority (50% + 1) in both the House of Clergy and the House of Laity in a majority of diocesan synods (i.e. in 23 or more). If it fails to get that number it will fail. However, if it does get a simple majority in at least 23 diocesan synods then it will be returned to the General Synod for final approval. But here it will need to get a 2/3 majority (66.6%) in all three Houses (Bishops, Clergy, Laity) in order to be passed and sent to the Parliament at Westminster for final approval.

The purpose of the Measure is to allow the General Synod "to make provision by canon for enabling a woman to be ordained to the office of priest". Yet included in the Measure as Part II are various provisions concerning what Bishops, parishes and cathedrals must declare and do. To the ordinary person these may seem very confusing and burdensome and sure to cause trouble and heartache, if and when they are implemented. Further, associated with the Measure (but not being voted upon in diocesan synods) is another piece of legislation (which will only need a simple majority in General Synod to be passed), known as the "Financial Provisions Measure". The purpose is to make provision for the relief of hardship of those clergy and church workers who resign their offices because they feel that the Church has acted contrary to the will of God in agreeing to the ordination of women as priests. By making this provision, those in favour of the "Priests (Ordination of Women) Measure" hope to remove an obstacle to its being passed. Thus until this Financial Measure is passed the major Measure on ordaining women cannot be voted on.

I hope this brief explanation makes it clear that the issue being voted upon is far more complex than whether or not a woman should be ordained as a priest in the Church of England. In fact some who think it right to ordain a woman may well vote against the legislation because they feel it is a sure way to create further and fixed divisions both in and between parishes and dioceses.

MAN WOMAN & PRIESTHOOD

If you would like to know more about the theological issues involved in female ordination, Gracewing the publishers of **Let Women be Women** also publish **Man, Woman & Priesthood** a collection of essays from across the churches by churchmen, theologians and lay people opposed to the ordination of women.

Contributors include **Graham Leonard,** Anglican Bishop of London; **Mary Kenny,** a prominent Catholic lay person; **J I Packer,** the well known evangelical writer; **James Tolhurst,** a Newman scholar; **Andrew McGowan,** a Presbyterian Minister; **Roman Cholij,** an Eastern Catholic theologian; and **Joyce Little,** an American nun and theologian.

In addition to the essays the book also includes the most important church documents on the subject from the Anglican, Catholic and Orthodox churches. An extensive bibliography is also provided for those who wish to study this subject in even more detail.

Paperback £7.95